A Widower's Walk:
From Desert to Destiny

By Danny White
LtCol, USMC (Ret.)

A Widower's Walk: From Desert to Destiny

Copyright © 2021 by Daniel F. White II (Danny White)

All rights reserved. No portion of this book may be reproduced in any form without written permission of the publisher. It is illegal to copy this book, post it to a web site, or distribute it by any other means without permission from the publisher.

Scripture quotations are taken from the Holy Bible.

Scriptures marked KJV are taken from the King James Version (KJV), public domain.

Scriptures marked NKJV are taken from the New King James Version ® Copyright ©1982, by Thomas Nelson. Used by permission.

Scriptures marked ESV are taken from the English Standard Version® (ESV®) Copyright © 2001 by Crossway, a publishing ministry of Good News Publishers. All rights reserved. Used by permission.

Scriptures marked CJB are taken from the COMPLETE JEWISH BIBLE (CJB): Scripture taken from the COMPLETE JEWISH BIBLE, copyright© 1998 by David H. Stern. Published by Jewish New Testament Publications, Inc. www.messianicjewish.net/ jntp. Distributed by Messianic Jewish Resources Int'l. www.messianicjewish.net. All rights reserved. Used by permission.

Cover Design: Brittney Bywater Design LLC

Original Photo: Cover Photo by Amy Hinds

ISBN 978-1-7355435-3-6

Printed and bound in the United States of America

Published by The Warrior's Journey in partnership with Three Clicks Publishing. 3003 East Chestnut Expressway Ste 2001 Springfield, MO 65802

Table of Contents

Endorsements	v
Acknowledgments	xv
Dedication	xvii
Foreword	xix
Introduction	xxi
Chapter 1: Learning to See Pictures	1
Chapter 2: Early Life	5
Chapter 3: Jenny ~ High School Sweetheart	11
Chapter 4: Marriage to Jenny	21
Chapter 5: A Growing Family	31
Chapter 6: The Day Life Changed	41
Chapter 7: It's NOT a Platitude… Positive Leadership Makes a Difference	47
Chapter 8: Pictures of Community	51
Chapter 9: Freedom in Finances	61
Chapter 10: Stay Marine?	65
Chapter 11: Easter ~ New Beginnings	95
Chapter 12: Courting Nora	105
Chapter 13: Marriage to Nora	117
Chapter 14: Chapter of Life with Nora Begins	121
Chapter 15: Career ~ Crash and Burn	139
Chapter 16: Two Life-Changing Questions	147
Chapter 17: Lead with Liberty Version 1.0	159
Conclusion	171
Postscript ~ Lead with Liberty Version 2.0	175

Endorsements

"Danny White has written a detailed account of how God will help us through the worst tragedies. The detail is a primer on decision making amidst pain one can't understand. This is a must read book for men, believers or not, who are trying to figure out what is important in life."

Maj Gen John S. Grinalds, USMC (Ret.)

"*A Widower's Walk* is a striking account of Danny White's journey in discipleship. I met Danny some years ago and was instantly struck by his passion to follow Jesus. I have seen the same devotion to duty, honor, and faithfulness in his journey that made him an exemplary Marine officer. Danny White's story is a contemporary study of a disciple of the Messiah. I was struck again and again by the relevance of following Jesus in sometimes very difficult circumstances. Anyone who reads this gripping account of his quest for victory in life will not put it down unchanged. It has been for me an encouragement to respond again to Jesus' command: 'Come, follow me.'"

Ray Vander Laan
Historian and Author of *That the World May Know Faith Lessons*

"In early 2018, I hosted Danny on The Warrior's Journey podcast for the first time. I had read his book *A Widower's Walk: From Desert to Destiny* prior to that conversation, yet was amazed at hearing him recount with our audience, with complete transparency, God's faithfulness to him through the pain of perhaps the biggest fear a husband and/or parent could have. He watched his pregnant wife Jenny and five-year old son Danny die in a single vehicle accident during a December 1997 military move.

Since that podcast, I've hosted him several other times, and each time the engagement from our listeners is among the highest we've seen, connecting powerfully with our audience. Danny brings a wealth of experiential wisdom gained through some dark nights of the soul with the deaths of Jenny and son Danny, plus other 'Purple Hearts' of suffering with his wife Nora's two miscarriages, his mother's death, and the passing of his 41-year-old brother.

With each different experienced tragedy, Danny has learned to lean more and more into his faith in Christ. God has shaped and equipped him to be an authentic communicator on the lessons learned about leadership, resiliency, finances, marriage struggles and joys, blended family issues, parenting, and other topics on everyday life.

I'm so impressed and inspired at how Danny remains pliable and teachable in the Master's hands. When I first met him, he was running Lead with Liberty as a business. Then in 2019, he felt directed by God to shut down the business and re-form Lead with Liberty as a non-profit ministry. I was struck by the peace that he had with this transition in spite of the uncertainty of leaving what he had known for seven years after retiring from active duty in the Marine Corps.

Danny has my highest endorsement to serve as a speaker for any organization, whether faith-based or secular. He's comfortable bringing the Truth with grace and humility to any audience and encouraging the listeners to look to God as the true source of resiliency through tough times or 'desert experiences' of life."

Kevin Weaver
President/CEO, The Warrior's Journey

"I have known the White family for many years; in fact, I prayed for Danny and Jon when they were boys at the Holmes Bible College Camp Meetings where I was speaking.

Even though I heard Danny share part of his story at the celebration of his retirement from the Marine Corps, the book held my attention, and I could not put it down until I had finished reading it. It is a fascinating book tracing Danny's journey through terrible tragedy to a deeper faith in God, to becoming a better husband and father, and to developing into a leader in the U.S. Marine Corps. The tragedy of watching in his rear view window as his wife's car wrecked is heart-wrenching. Yet he walked through that valley of despair with faith to continue his career to become a Lt. Col. in the Marine Corps.

The book is both inspirational and instructional. It is full of practical advice for men about discovering who they are and how they should relate to others, especially to one's wife and children. The lessons on leadership are invaluable. These lessons Danny shares in his conferences on "*LEADING WITH LIBERTY.*"

The Late Bishop James D. Leggett
Former President of Holmes Bible College
Former Presiding Bishop of International Pentecostal Holiness Church

"In 1992, I met Danny at Camp Lejeune, North Carolina where we both were attending our training to become Marine Corps combat engineer officers. Then we were stationed together in Okinawa, Japan at the same unit for three years. We were running partners, and our families spent time in each other's homes. Our paths crossed again in 1998 when we attended the U.S. Army Engineer Officer Advanced Course in Fort

Leonard Wood, Missouri.

Upon hearing about Danny's pregnant wife Jenny and five-year-old son Little Danny passing during a 1997 military move, I was heartbroken for him and wondered how he was doing. My wife and I traveled to South Carolina to attend the funerals and be with Danny and his two surviving children.

To see his faith and trust in God was inspiring and encouraging. I have shared Danny's story countless times since 1997 with other Marines, and many were deeply moved by this man's faith and hope in the LORD. Though not a perfect man, Danny's relationship with God has continued to grow deeper and deeper as he has found God to be the Marine Corps motto *Semper Fidelis* ('Always Faithful') with each additional trial in life.

I was blessed to hear how Danny obeyed the LORD to shut down the business he founded after retiring from the Marine Corps, Lead with Liberty, and re-form it as a non-profit ministry. His heart is to be generous in sharing with others the experiential wisdom God has taught him through the years—just as God has been generous to him. I truly believe that Danny's story is one that will encourage many to turn to God during life's trials and find Him to be the *God of all comfort* to them just like He was to Danny."

Semper Fidelis,
Dwayne Whiteside
Colonel, U.S. Marine Corps (Ret.)

"This book will bring about joy, laughter, sorrow, and personal reflection as you read the life story of retired USMC Lt. Colonel Danny White. By sharing his story, Danny leaves each reader with having to answer life's two greatest questions: Who are you? What are you doing here? These two questions will take each reader to a deeper reflection on how they would answer these after reading about Danny's life. I would highly recommend Danny as a guest speaker for your church, civic group, or gathering, and after reading his book, I believe you will as well.

"I would be more than happy to discuss my friend Danny White with you if you have any questions. I can be reached by contacting me by phone @ 864-269-2114 or by e-mail @ talkwithbrad@gmail.com."

Rev. William Brad Atkins, Sr.
Senior Pastor of Lake Bowen Baptist Church
2012 President of the South Carolina Baptist Convention

"A must read for anyone who has ever felt like they are losing their marbles. Danny has trudged through hot desert sands on life's journey. His ability to be transparent and 'real' offers hope and encouragement to tired, thirsty souls."

Deborah Osterhoudt
Wife of retired U.S. Army Officer

"Meeting Danny White is a real privilege; but hearing his testimony and finding out what God has done in and through his life is a true honor. Brother Danny's life story is one that will have you crying from a broken heart one moment—then the very next moment shouting from that same heart for the victory that God has blessed him with in life. Having such a decorated man in both the United States Military and in God's Army will only encourage you to Lead with Liberty in your own life. Danny is a true testimony to what God can do with a heart that has been completely surrendered to HIM! His message will encourage, inspire, and empower the heart of any man that reads it and learns from it. Danny is the true picture of a mighty man by leading with a humble spirit. You will be blessed to know him…a common man with an extraordinary story about an amazing God"

Dr. Brad Kelley
Senior Pastor, Shiloh Baptist Church, NC
Former 1st and 2nd Vice President of the South Carolina Baptist Convention

"Every man has a story, and every man's story is worth the telling and is worth the hearing. Such is certainly the case with Danny's story and the journey of faith he has been on so far. He has told his story powerfully, with candor and a vulnerability that will draw the readers into seeing perhaps their own stories in a new perspective. His story is one of great tragedy, a tragedy almost too difficult to comprehend. Yet, it is also a story of triumph, a triumph experienced because of a deep and abiding faith in Jesus and a resounding confidence that tragedy is not beyond the love of Jesus. Danny brings the reader face to face with the reality that suffering is part of life and it is through the doors of suffering the love of Jesus is experienced in ways not otherwise possible."

John E. Bishop
Marine and Businessman

"*A Widower's Walk* is the amazing story of how Danny, and his family, live out the Scripture, 'My grace is sufficient for you.' An inspiring message of hope and renewal for those seeking a breakthrough in their lives. A must read for all who are called to lead their families and balance the demands of everyday living."

Michael Osterhoudt
Elder & Men's Ministry Leader
Northern Virginia

"I've served with Danny and been privileged to share his friendship since 1999. *A Widower's Walk: From Desert to Destiny* is an inspiring as it is compelling account of Danny's personal traverse through tragedy, grief, despair, hope, and happiness and an exposé of one man and his family's ability to find resilience through their faith, trust in themselves and those close to them, and the support of dedicated leaders. It also highlights, at the personal level, a variety of leadership lessons, central to them being the importance of reconciling one's relationship with one's self such that you truly 'know' yourself before pursuing an aspiration to positively lead others. It was this foundational premise that underpinned my leadership addresses to Australian Army Officer Cadets during my time as Commandant of the Royal Military College, Duntroon."

David M. Luhrs
Brigadier, Australian Army (Retired)

"Lead with Liberty"–A German Perspective

"Already back in the early '90s, I realized that the commitment Americans have in their church and also the way they share their life with God is so much different from the German—and likely many other European countries'—Christian practise. Neither better nor worse, just different. Along with my two years of flying training in California and while participating in numerous exercises in the U.S. or together with U.S. Air Force Squadrons, I learned that church in the U.S. is a very prominent topic: for example, during a casual office chat, where you just talk about current church activities or about last Sunday's sermon. Well, this just doesn't happen in a *Luftwaffe* Squadron or most other German offices. Although surprising and sometimes unfamiliar, I didn't really think about those differences a lot.

"This, however, changed when I started my tour as a German Liaison Officer to the U.S. Joint Staff J-3 at the Pentagon in 2008—when I met Danny White as a colleague and comrade in the office. My predecessor on the job told me about the tragedy, which struck the White family so mercilessly back in 1997—and my first thought was: 'How can you ever handle a situation like this without losing your mind...?' During the following three years of my assignment, over many lunch breaks and during business trips or dinner invitations, I listened and learned how it worked for my colleague and friend Danny—how he did not lose his mind, and much more found new meaning in life with his dear wife Nora. I was amazed not only by the importance of church, of trust and belief in God, but also by the way senior U.S. Marine Corps officers lived their military leadership and took personal care of a stumbling fellow Marine. Danny White describes these different dimensions of help and support quite excellently in his book. So reading it brought back memories of our many conversations, but it also added details and thoughts I was yet not aware of.

"Altogether I could now explain to a German how a friend of mine dealt with an unbelievably hard and tragic moment in his life and how the different U.S. 'approach' to church and God helped him to survive in a straightforward manner. Did I however change my personal Christian life? Did I adopt a more American style? Well, I have to admit, probably not. But I took a most important lesson with me, a lesson that should be in the hip pocket of every leader, especially every military leader: Leadership goes so far beyond reaching objectives and fulfilling tasks and missions. As a military leader, you not only have to be aware of your soldiers' sorrows and troubles—you have to engage in helping them through those rough times. Helping them in a way as Danny describes as providing them a picture. This for me in turn means, as a leader your help should not be limited to words and reason. Your help should be contributing and at best be the picture—so that those in need can find a hook to hang onto.

"Thank you Danny for adding this most valuable insight to my military toolbox!"

Michael "T-man" Trautermann
Colonel, *Luftwaffe* (German Air Force)

"The story of Danny White is only one man's story. Or is it really? How many of us, by exchanging our own personal facts with his, could feel with him the deserts, the losses, the tragedies, and the desperate climb seeking the commendation of men? Reaching the top of that voracious pursuit, we also have found ourselves alone on a foggy peak and no clear pathway beyond. You will be deeply touched by Danny's story, as was I. Be certain that the God he clung to in his story also keeps all of your tears in his bottle. This fact will encourage you to follow Danny's hard-won leadership and begin to be aware of 'first things' as well. Thus begins true liberty as you also climb a hill called Mt. Calvary and leave self there at the foot of the Cross. Only then was Danny's true pathway clear. Thank you, Danny, for sharing your journey, your story. May we choose to be the wiser for it.

Mrs. Judy Rae Carlson
Author; Homemaker and Wife of 52 years

"Danny White is a strong leader whose intimate story includes the ups and downs of real life. It is an inspiring account of achievement and redemption, told in an honest and transparent way. From triumph to tragedy and back again, as a father, husband, and military leader, he has a great deal to say that will touch each of us in some way."

Eric Pillmore
Former Senior Vice President–Corporate Governance,
Tyco International

Acknowledgments

To God who has been—and continues to be—the Marine Corps motto *Semper Fidelis* ("Always Faithful") to my family and me. He's the reason for this story. Even though written in the first person, the intent of this story is to brag on Him, not me.

To those who, since 1998, heard part of this story and wanted to know more.

To Larry Steve Crain, an Army veteran, for sharing his time and talent to initially shape this story in 2001, as a magazine article, then to edit the first printing manuscript even while carrying a rucksack filled with other responsibilities. His detailed questions helped add ligaments and muscles to the skeleton and significantly improved each subsequent version.

To Deborah Osterhoudt for graciously providing a detailed review of the first printing manuscript and providing a lady's perspective. Her insights greatly enhanced this story to better glorify the LORD. Also, many thanks for her help to design the logo for Lead with Liberty Ministries.

To Marianne Ward for selflessly editing the first printing manuscript to improve the presentation of the message. And for believing in this story—and that it needed to be told.

To Amy Hinds for her time and talents to re-do the front cover for the second printing (amyhindsphotography.shootproof.com).

To Nora, my bride, for her support and encouragement: stay the course…don't quit. She provided her thoughts about marrying a widower and the struggles we've faced in our marriage—which proved to enrich much of the story's behind-the-scenes. Nora, I love you. You truly are the demonstration of the LORD's favor as found in Proverbs 18:22 (ESV): "He who finds a wife finds a good thing and obtains favor from the LORD."

The facts of this story are taken from my memory, journals, and letters. Any errors are due to omission rather than commission.

This story reflects my views and does not necessarily represent the views of the Department of Defense or the U.S. Marine Corps.

Dedication

This book is dedicated to the LORD and His glory.
And to the community He used to give me
courage in the deserts of life.
If just one detail had unfolded differently,
this story would have died in the desert.

Foreword

Gripping. Moving. I read this book in a single sitting, seeing my own spiritual journey in its pages! Danny White achieved the rank of Lieutenant Colonel of Marines, has a beautiful wife, and a quiver full of delightful children. At first glance, he appears to be the prince in a "happily ever after" fairytale—a man living the American dream. But his happiness has been forged in the fires of hardship and his character has been hammered out on the anvil of adversity.

He spoke in my church while the deaths of his first wife, firstborn son, and unborn child were burning in his soul, testing his faith like few of us have ever been tested, and I marveled at his testimony of God's sustaining grace. His story of how the Lord brought him through the pain and into the joy of a new marriage reads like a modern-day book of Job. Like Job, Danny thrives today because he is anchored on the courage-giving truth that nothing happens to him that does not pass though the hands of a sovereign, good God who can be (and must be) trusted even when we don't understand His ways.

Never presenting himself as the hero of the story, Danny humbly admits his failures as a Christian, a husband, and a father on his "every man's journey" toward realizing the reality of Christ and beginning a legacy of living for a higher purpose than just working for personal advancement. He does it in a way that all men can relate to and learn from because all men come sort of the glory of God and grow weary at their repeated failures to balance faith, family fitness, and work.

In these pages, Danny unfolds a pathway to the power of God available to every man who knows Christ, giving the glory to the Lord who mentored him to the point where he is now requested to give "seminars of hope" to all men who want to be what only God can make them.

This book encourages the soul; it refreshes the spirit. Enjoy.

Pastor Brad Lapiska, Colonel, USMC (Ret.)

Introduction

Remember. Remember. Remember.

Remember is a powerful word. You may recall a significant date in your life by reflecting on where you were and what you were doing. A few of you may remember where you were when you heard about the Japanese attack on Pearl Harbor on December 7, 1941. More will remember where you were on November 22, 1963, when you heard that John F. Kennedy was assassinated. Many will recall what you were doing on September 11, 2001, when you first heard about multiple terrorist attacks carried out on our nation's soil.

Other dates became milestones in your life—and the rest of the world is likely unaware of their significances. December 14, 1997, was such a day for me.

That day, en route from Bridgeport, California, to Fort Leonard Wood, Missouri, I looked in my rearview mirror and watched my pregnant wife, Jenny, and our five-year-old son, Danny, die in a single-vehicle accident. My *squared-away* world shattered and disintegrated in mere seconds. One minute, I, a Marine Corps captain, was on my way to attend a military school; the next minute, my high school sweetheart, our firstborn son, and our unborn baby were dead.

I remember wondering helplessly, *Why did this happen? What will I do? Is there any way I can be a single-parent to three-year-old*

Hannah and nine-month-old Ethan and still serve as a Marine? Will I make it through this "desert experience"? How?

People deal with desert experiences in many different ways. Some opt to escape the pain-by ending their earthly lives. They fear their circumstances more than they fear death. It is impossible to fully understand what goes through their minds during their final moments, but it is doubtful that they truly consider the resulting desert experiences they will put their loved ones through.

Others use alcohol or drugs to cope with pain, but the anticipated relief is only temporary. The potential effects of either choice can spiral downward and cause a desert experience to worsen.

Some seek help from counselors, as they realize that, on their own, they don't have answers. Others turn to their *communities,* groups of caring people gleaned from among their families, friends, neighborhoods, and churches.

Another way I've seen people deal with desert experiences involves turning to their faith journeys and seeking help from God.

I wrestled with all those options—and the consequences of each—after that horrible accident on an Arizona highway in 1997. I thought back over the life I'd experienced before tragedy struck. For the first time, I began to see *pictures* from my life—pictures that helped me see deeper truths.

CHAPTER 1
Learning to See Pictures

As a Marine Corps captain, I learned to see the pictures that are in the Bible (or the *Text*) from the Rev. Ray Vander Laan (RVL) through a home Bible study group at Fort Leonard Wood, Missouri, in April 1998. In that study group, we used *That the World May Know Faith Lessons* (www.followtherabbi.com), which took my faith journey to a new level. After several lessons, I was hooked by RVL's insights and purchased the entire series.

RVL became a mentor along my faith journey, and during a later seminar, RVL shared another picture from the Text that became a milestone along my faith journey. He related this vignette:

A man named Ben, while traveling in Israel, went to visit his friend, a rabbi. Walking into the rabbi's office, Ben saw a humongous, beautiful glass jar, filled with an amazing rainbow of marbles, sitting on the rabbi's desk. In jest, he asked the rabbi, "What are you doing? Playing marbles with your disciples?"

The rabbi smiled and said, "No," and then quoted in Hebrew Psalm 90:12 (KJV): "So teach us to number our days, that we may apply our hearts unto wisdom."

The rabbi paused and continued, "After hearing those words, I wanted to have a picture of what *numbering my days* meant. Mulling over the thought, I considered my family tree and how long my grandparents and great-grandparents had lived. Taking a calculated guess on my life expectancy, I determined how many days I already had lived and then estimated how many days I had left. I bought that number of marbles and this jar.

"Each morning I take a marble from the jar and have a conversation with God: 'LORD, I bless You for this day. Please help me to honor You. Please guide me as I meet with Mr. Schmedlap, as he can be difficult to work with. Help my words to honor You while teaching my disciples.' I put the marble in my pocket and proceed with the day as planned.

"At the end of the day, I take the marble out and have a 'debriefing' time with God: 'LORD, I bless You for Your help today. Please forgive me for not being loving, like You, toward Mr. Schmedlap. I bless You for helping me instruct my disciples.' After praying, I throw the marble away. Day by day, the level of marbles in the jar decreases, giving me a picture—and a reminder—that I'm not getting any more marbles or days in my life."

RVL paused and asked if we saw the picture. Stunned at seeing the picture, I realized I had squandered many, many marbles—and would never get them back. As I mulled over that picture, the blinding-flash-of-the-obvious hit me: Based on my gene pool, I had less than half of my total days worth of marbles left! What would I do with what remained? I could get more money and things but couldn't get more time. Then, like a laser beam, the corollary to that thought struck me: The most precious gift anyone can give is his or her time!

I should have paid attention to Psalm 90:12 while reading it as a child. I longed to be able to hit *Stop*, *Rewind*, and then *Play* for many of my marbles.

LEARNING TO SEE PICTURES

I now keep a marble in my truck as a reminder, when looking down at the cup holder: *Remember to be wise in how you spend the time you've been given today*.

My thoughts then drifted to my childhood days, back when my jar was full of *marbles*....

A WIDOWER'S WALK

CHAPTER 2

Early Life

I was born in 1969 to Frank and Myrtle White and grew up in the rural Mountain View Community of Greenville County, South Carolina. My dad (*Daddy*) was the fifth child of six children. He grew up in the same community and played a trombone in the Blue Ridge High School band and continued playing for churches he attended.

Daddy worked in maintenance at Allen Bennett Hospital in Greer, South Carolina, for ten years and then worked as a cable splicer for Southern Bell Telephone and Telegraph Company's work center in Greenville, South Carolina, for over nineteen years. His supervisors at Southern Bell sent him on the most tedious projects to ensure that they were completed correctly and not in a slipshod manner. Daddy took early retirement after the proliferation of fiber optic cable. My dad did not allow a television or junk food in our house while we were growing up. He also insisted that nothing be wasted. We gave him a funny sign with this proclamation: "Use it up. Wear it out. Eat it all."

My mom (*Mama*) grew up as the older daughter of a U.S. Army enlisted soldier and graduated from Mecklenburg High School in Charlotte, North Carolina. After moving to Greenville, South Carolina, both her parents worked full-time at a textile mill until they both reached retirement age. Mama worked as an AT&T operator until my sister was born. She then worked as a stay-at-home mom and worked harder at home than she did any day at AT&T.

My parents instilled a solid work ethic in my younger siblings—Jonathan (*Jon*), born in 1971, and Jane, born in 1972—and me. We learned how to raise our own food in a half-acre sized subsistence garden and care for horses, cows, and goats as well as cut firewood on the 29-plus acres my parents owned. Mama had an old cowbell she used to page us from the back part of the property: when we heard the bell ring, we knew we'd better head back to the house. One time, we failed to logically connect our response, and when we returned, we found that Mama was rather irate.

"Danny, where were *you three*?" she asked. (Because I was the oldest, Mama frequently referred to me as *Danny, you three*.)

"We only heard the cow bell the third time!" I said.

Oops! Our hearing and response time greatly improved after a counseling session from Mama.

As we grew older, many of our friends leaped at opportunities to come out to the country and spend part of a day with us to: ride our horse, Dolly; walk in the woods; sit on our front porch and look at an incredible view of the Blue Ridge Mountains; or go for a hayride in our trailer built from scratch by our dad and his dad and pulled by a Case tractor.

My dad's parents lived down the hill from us, approximately one thousand yards away, in *The Old Home-Place*. My dad's mom and her family moved into The Old Home-Place in 1919, when she was nine years old. She had five sisters and four brothers. *Papa White*, as we called my dad's father, was one of the hardest-working men I've ever known. Like Paul Bunyan, he split wood with an ax and hit the same crack every time. We enjoyed riding home with him from church on Sunday nights; he drove fast—*like a scalded dog*, to our delight—and gave us his favorite candy, Butterfinger® candy bars, from the glove compartment of his grey Chevrolet Caprice.

Papa White passed away in 1985, and my brother Jon and I, along with our male cousins, served as pallbearers at his funeral at Gum Springs Pentecostal Holiness Church. I still miss him.

Another favorite pastime for my siblings and me was spending Friday nights with my mom's parents, *Mima* and *Grandpa*, and Mama's sister, *Aunt Val*, who lived with them at that time. Their house was loaded with a varied assortment of junk food, and we were allowed to watch movies and TV as late as we wanted to. On Saturday mornings when we stayed at their home, they prepared sumptuous breakfasts of bacon, sausage, scrambled eggs (to this day, I haven't found anyone who can cook fluffy, tender scrambled eggs quite like Mima could), grits, and biscuits. Amazing aromas drew us to their table from our late-night stupors. Stuffed with delicious Southern cooking, we would zone into food-induced comas and nap until early afternoon before preparing for our trip back home. We truly enjoyed being the only three grandchildren on my mom's side.

My parents sacrificed financially to send the three of us, from kindergarten through twelfth grade, to Hampton Park Christian School (HPCS) in Greenville, South Carolina. Looking back, I see that my parents gave up many things to invest in solid educational foundations for us. Also, I owe much to the superb teachers at HPCS who also sacrificed by working for less pay in order to invest in their future generations. Many of the skills I learned at HPCS—public speaking, writing, and math, to name a few—helped set me up for success as a Marine.

Our parents cultivated a love of music in my siblings and me. Mama played the piano beautifully at home and for churches she attended. She drove Jon, Jane, and me to piano lessons each week for nine years. My siblings and I learned to play trombones and played in the HPCS high school band. Also the three of us took voice lessons from Mrs. Ina Pegram. For two years I took voice lessons (which later played a part in this story).

Daddy and Mama also instilled a solid foundation for our faith journeys. We had family devotions in the evenings, and as we learned to read, we took part in reading the Bible, verse by verse. I accepted Jesus Christ as Lord and Savior at eight years of age. I matured gradually along my faith journey and began having my own quiet time of reading the Bible and praying.

During my childhood, we attended Gum Springs Pentecostal Holiness Church, located less than two miles from our home. Jon, Jane, and I ran around outside the church building after services—we were forbidden to run inside after one futile attempt—and we dared each other and our friends to go into the church's cemetery at night.

Neither of my parents felt an obligation to be an ATM machine for our spending money. Therefore, we found a way to earn spending money by cutting grass and raking leaves. During summers, when Jane, Jon, and I were around ages nine, eleven, and thirteen, we began to help our dad mow, using push mowers, the grass at the parsonage and around the church building, including the dreaded cemetery.

As I grew into adolescence and then my teen years, I spent my efforts seeking affirmation from others in order to *scratch an itch*: I didn't realize that my father was proud of me. Affirming words were scarce in his upbringing. I threw myself into my studies in high school and strove for academic success. My senior year of high school I pursued a Naval Reserve Officers Training Corps (NROTC) Marine-option scholarship in order to join the Marine Corps—the toughest organization I knew of—largely to prove to my father and the rest of the world that I was a man.

Then I met an amazing young lady.

CHAPTER 3

Jenny ~ High School Sweetheart

The voice of an angel echoed through the halls of Anderson College. Powering that voice was Jennifer (*Jenny*) Shaw, the most beautiful woman I had ever seen. I racked my brain for ways to get her attention and notice me. Summoning my high school senior courage, I did the *logical* thing: I threw acorns at her.

When she tried to return fire and missed, repeatedly, I laughed … and was smitten.

An eternity passed (actually, only one week) and there sat Mrs. Frankie Shaw, Jenny's mom, in her gray Volkswagen van at HPCS, waiting to pick up Jenny's four younger sisters from school.

"Hello, Mrs. Shaw. How are you today?"

"Great, Danny. It's good to see you."

"I think I went overboard in teasing Jenny at the voice competition last week. Would you mind giving me your phone number, so I could call her and apologize?"

"Oh, Jenny had a great time. She's not upset at you."

"Well, would you mind giving me your number, so I can make sure?"

With my high school voice faltering, as much as my bravado, I placed the call.

"Hello, Jenny. This is Danny White."

"Hi, Danny."

"I just wanted to make sure I hadn't hurt your feelings by teasing you and throwing acorns at you. I'm concerned that I went too far."

"You didn't. I thought it was funny. Thanks for calling to check."

"So you're sure I didn't hurt your feelings?"

"Yes, I'm sure."

"Well, I just wanted to make sure."

"Thanks again. Sorry, but I have to go."

That's it! The call was over . . . way too soon for me. A few calls later I finally asked her out. To my surprise, she said I needed to ask her dad for permission. Not one to shrink from a challenge, yet with fear and trembling, I made an appointment to call Mr. David Shaw in order to request his permission to take Jenny on a date, and, to my relief, he gave his approval.

For our first date, my planning prowess was lacking—remember, at that point I wasn't a Marine, yet. I invited Jenny to attend *The Wizard of Oz,* a play in which I was playing the Tin Man. Actors had to arrive two hours early for stage set-up and make-up. So, instead of having a *normal* date, the Shaws brought Jenny to the play.

The night before our date, I threatened to throw acorns at Jenny during the play performance—and she believed I would do it! I didn't, only because I feared my attempts to tease Jenny might be reflected in my final drama grade at HPCS.

In my haste and anticipation of that first date, I failed to remember a towel and shower gear. After the play, I walked Jenny to my parents' tan 1966 Ford Fairlane, opened the passenger door, and helped her in. Then carefully driving at the speed limit, lest we attract the attention of a police officer who would wonder why a crazy-looking guy in silver paint was chauffeuring a rather beautiful and normal-looking young lady, I drove Jenny home. Fortunately we made it to the Shaw house without incident.

JENNY~ HIGH SCHOOL SWEETHEART

Amazingly Jenny agreed to go out with me again. And again.

During my 1987 graduation from high school, the Marine Corps presented me a four-year NROTC Marine-option scholarship. As the audience applauded, it wasn't only my parents' approval I wanted—I knew my mom was proud of me. I will always remember scanning the sea of faces hurriedly, for Jenny. Once I saw her, we locked eyes—and time stopped as she smiled proudly at me. At that moment, thoughts simultaneously bombarded me—and one that kept repeating itself: *She's the one for me.*

I chose to attend The Citadel in Charleston, South Carolina. Freshman year or *knob[1] year* was a challenge: mentally, emotionally, and physically. I reported in at six feet, three inches tall and 175 pounds and sheltered by my upbringing. I heard cursing for the first time almost the moment the knob check-in process began.

Jenny, then a high school senior at Bob Jones Academy, faithfully wrote letters to me, which helped me keep going, one day at a time. Every letter made a difference in my day—to see a letter from her in my Citadel P.O. box, rather than the standard *airmail* (a cadet term for no mail ... only a blast of air hitting one's face after opening the tiny door of the P.O. box). Jenny wrote about how she was looking forward to graduating from high school and making plans to attend Bob Jones University (BJU). She told me about her determination to complete a challenging math problem with the necessary proofs. She loved the subject and wanted to become a high school math teacher. Jenny thrived on being recognized by a teacher for her diligent work, and to her, that made all the effort worthwhile. I learned from reading her letters that she was eager to go *above and beyond* to please those who were dear to her and that it was difficult to say

---

1   Freshmen at The Citadel are called *knobs* because their shaved heads look like doorknobs.

"No" because it was seen as letting someone down and that was unacceptable and a failure. Jenny's correspondence reflected that when she made a friend, it was for life—and that she would make a concerted effort to maintain that friendship regardless of the miles that might separate her from that friend. I discovered her ability to find something in each person she met that she could relate to, that she could like about them. She wrote about the hilarious events that happened at her work—initially a fast food restaurant, then a Christian bookstore. Her delightful laughter *echoed off* the pages as she described a skit that went haywire at school, something comical at work, or her excitement at making a craft and sharing it with others.

I leaned daily on the LORD to help with challenges during that academic year. Since freshmen were not allowed to have phones in our rooms until second semester, my letter writing improved as I attempted to return the favor to Jenny.

Toward the end of my knob year, I traveled home to see Jenny and attended Hampton Park Baptist Church's (HPBC) Wednesday evening service with her. I knew many people at HPBC since the church sponsored the school (HPCS). One person in particular at HPBC I specifically looked for and greeted was Mrs. Ina Pegram. I wanted to acknowledge, in some way, my appreciation for her voice lessons that introduced Jenny to me.

After that Wednesday evening service, Jenny introduced me to Hampton Park's then-new youth pastor, Marine Corps Captain Brad Lapiska, an AH-1 Cobra helicopter pilot. Brad had just transitioned from active duty to the Marine Corps Reserve in order to answer God's call to attend seminary at BJU and ultimately become a preacher. (His Marine aviation call sign was *Preacher*.) This professional Marine—a godly *man's man*—deeply impressed me, and I felt grateful that we clicked right away. He offered to meet with me any time I was available when home from college. His mentoring and advice since 1988 have proven to be invaluable to me as a Marine, husband, and father.

After completing my knob year, I reported for a three-week training session and then a four-week session (both in Charleston), as part of my NROTC scholarship. Jenny and I continued to learn how to maintain our long-distance relationship throughout the summer. She did not give up on our relationship during what would later be judged as an *easy* time (a time of NROTC demands on me) compared to subsequent demands the Marine Corps placed on my life. I learned that coming home was a very sweet and precious time—that perception proved to be true, deployment after deployment, during my Calling #1.[2]

My sophomore year began with my heading back early to The Citadel to help train an incoming freshman class and serve as our cadre Company Clerk. My academic major in Civil Engineering proved to be a challenge, for, as a cadet, one must balance academics with a military lifestyle: formations, drills, parades, uniform preparation, *white-glove* inspections, and physical fitness. I began to get off course in my faith journey, and felt I could make it on my own. Since my knob year was over, I acted as if God was now an option. Oh, how wrong I was! Ever so slowly, I began to get off balance in my life, focusing on the *physical leg*—being in shape—and the *mental leg* (academics) but neglecting the *spiritual leg*. Think of a three-legged stool, with one leg almost non-existent.

During the summer of 1989, I reported for four weeks of NROTC training—one week each in: Pensacola, Florida; Charleston, South Carolina; Norfolk, Virginia; and Little Creek, Virginia.

---

2 I believe that God called me to serve a career in the Marine Corps—hence the term "Calling #1."

Upon returning to The Citadel at the beginning of my junior year, I had to select a *community* for my active duty service after graduation: the U.S. Navy (surface warfare, submarine, or aviation) or the Marines. This decision would focus my last two years of NROTC classes: Navy or Marine Corps. Still wanting to be a Marine, I signed on the dotted line and committed to serve in the Corps.

In September, The Citadel's Corps of Cadets struggled with a curveball: Hurricane Hugo made landfall over Charleston and destroyed much in its path as it moved inland into North Carolina. We cadets were sent away from The Citadel for three weeks, and our academic year changed significantly.

In May 1990, after completing my junior year, I went home for about three weeks and enjoyed time with Jenny and then attended summer school at The Citadel to lighten my senior year's academic load. One weekend, while in summer school, I borrowed a friend's car and drove to Greenville to see my family and Jenny, before she went on a BJU-sponsored choir tour to England and Ireland. After summer school and a week off in July, I reported to Officer Candidates School (OCS) in Quantico, Virginia. Those six-weeks of training aid in the screening of potential Marine Corps officers. Each candidate is assessed for the ability to lead Marines—which is an almost sacred privilege: being entrusted with leading America's sons and daughters. Think of it as officer boot camp.

My parents and siblings and Jenny with her family drove to Quantico to attend my OCS graduation on Friday, August 24. On Sunday night I returned to Charleston to begin my senior year. I remember thinking, *Hey! When do Jenny and I get to see each other?*

In October, we seniors received our Citadel rings and prepared to enter the *Long Gray Line* of alumni who preceded us. I escorted my mom and Jenny for the Ring Ceremony, and, again, felt mesmerized at how beautiful Jenny appeared as we walked through a huge replica of The Citadel ring. That evening, I surprised her with a miniature of my Citadel ring, and offered it as a promise ring. She graciously accepted it.

The academic year whirled by in a blur, and I (still six feet, three inches tall) filled out to 195 pounds. In May 1991, I found myself on a Saturday morning in The Citadel's full-dress salt and pepper uniform, marching across the stage to shake The Citadel president's (a retired three-star Air Force general) hand and receive my diploma. An hour later, I had changed from my Citadel graduation uniform into the Marine Corps dress blue uniform with Sam Browne belt and was standing at the front doors of The Citadel's Summerall Chapel, ready to be commissioned as a Second Lieutenant. Jenny told me later that she looked up and saw me standing in the front door entrance, as sunlight streamed into the dark chapel. This painful realization hit her: In a few minutes she was going to have to *let me go,* for after I received my commission, the Corps would be calling the shots in my life, as well as in hers, if we married.

We enjoyed a few days together, going on walks and sharing lunch or dinner before I drove to Quantico to attend The Basic School (TBS). TBS is a six-month school that all Marine Corps officers attend. There, they learn how to lead infantry platoons into combat. Based on each officer's performance at TBS, he or she is assigned a "military occupational specialty" (MOS), based on the needs of the Marine Corps. I felt grateful to receive my first choice of MOS: Combat Engineer Officer (MOS 1302).

Before leaving for TBS, I met with Brad Lapiska who had been promoted to the rank of major and had recently returned from Operations Desert Shield/Desert Storm. He gave me an unforgettable piece of advice: "Danny, you're going to serve with many different leaders. Each will have his or her style of leadership. Pay attention to each one, for you can learn as much about leadership from a bad leader as you can from a good one. So take notes." Thus began my study of leadership in the intense laboratory known as the U.S. Marine Corps.

During TBS, I drove to South Carolina for the July 4th long weekend and took Jenny's parents to lunch. I asked their permission to marry her. (Jenny knew that was the reason I had traveled to South Carolina that weekend.) They said, "Yes!"—and I was grateful beyond words.

I plotted how to *pop the question* to Jenny in a memorable way. My first plan was to ask her at the Battery in Charleston, where we had taken many walks during my years at The Citadel, but I could not calculate a plan to get her from Greenville to Charleston without arousing her suspicions. Finally, I conspired with Mr. Shaw to take her to Anderson College—where I had thrown acorns at her during the voice competition event—on a Saturday in September 1991. Her father told Jenny that a friend of his boss wanted to talk with her in Anderson—and, for the record, I did know Mr. Shaw's boss.

For once, when it mattered, my planning went perfectly. I told Jenny I was busy that weekend and thought it would be a stretch to see her. She was disappointed, thinking I was not making plans to see her that weekend. I headed to South Carolina on Friday evening and drove directly to my parents' home—a variation of my typical sequence: to see Jenny first and then go to my parents' house. As the sun rose on Saturday morning, I drove toward Anderson College. My mom had contacted campus security in advance to let them know of my plans and had asked them not to be alarmed when a Marine officer with a sheathed sword appeared on campus that morning. He was coming in peace—with a marriage proposal.

I parked my red 1990 GMC Jimmy out of sight from the parking lot where Mr. Shaw and I had agreed to meet. Dressed in my Marine Corps dress blue uniform, replete with one ribbon and marksmanship badges, Sam Browne belt and officer's Mameluke sword, I walked up to the Shaws' gray Volkswagen van. Merely yards away, I saw Jenny rubbing her eyes, completely oblivious to my presence in South Carolina. When she looked up and saw me at the van's sliding door, her eyes widened, and she smiled and asked incredulously, "What are you doing here?"

I said, "I have something to ask you, Ma'am. Would you take a walk with me?"

She started shaking. We walked down a path, and I pulled out the diamond ring and said, "I don't have much to offer you, but I want to spend my life with you. Would you do me the honor of marrying me?"

Her eyes lit up and her smile seemed like a sunbeam to me when she said, "Yes!"

I somehow managed to get the diamond on her left hand and on the correct finger.

We went out for dinner that evening after her BJU society meeting. On Sunday, we attended the morning service with my mom and siblings at Holmes Memorial Church (a church in Greenville, South Carolina, that we had attended since 1982) and announced our engagement. After a multitude of congratulations, we ate lunch together, and then, while taking her home before starting to return to Quantico, I spontaneously asked Jenny if she would like me to go to HPBC's evening service with her. Her face lit up with a smile as she said, "Yes!"

After all the congratulations from our friends at Hampton Park, I experienced a late launch-time and headed north on I-85 to I-95. Even though tired upon arriving at Quantico, I knew that delaying my departure in order to take Jenny to Hampton Park was more than worth it, for the smile on Jenny's face seemed to be permanent. Plus, *You only get engaged once,* I thought.

CHAPTER 4

Marriage to Jenny

After graduating from TBS, I took military leave (vacation time) over Thanksgiving 1991 to see my family and Jenny and then reported to the Marine Corps Engineer School (MCES) at Courthouse Bay, Camp Lejeune, North Carolina. I drove to South Carolina for Christmas, which landed mid-week that year. With only two days off (from noon on Tuesday to noon on Thursday), Jenny and I attempted to set a date and make tentative plans for our wedding. We had dreamed of a mid-May 1992 wedding after she graduated from college. But the Marine Corps decided differently: my orders directed me to report in early May to Okinawa, an island forming part of the Ryukyu Island archipelago. I had *unaccompanied* orders to Okinawa, Japan, for a 12-month tour. In order for Jenny to go overseas with me, we would have to get married, produce a certificate of marriage and request a change of orders to an *accompanied* tour—all before I graduated from MCES in April. Or, we could wait to get married until I returned from 12 months in Okinawa.

Jenny wanted to proceed with getting married and requesting the change of orders in hopes that we could begin our married life in the Corps, sooner rather than later. Initially our hastened plans took her parents by storm. Finally convincing her mom this was not an excuse to elope, we selected Friday, February 14, 1992, for our wedding, since I would have a long weekend for President's Day. At that time, BJU did not allow students to get married while school was in session. Yet again, Brad Lapiska helped us immensely. He approached BJU on our behalf to validate Jenny's request to get married during her senior year and vouch for our unusual situation. BJU allowed Jenny to marry me before she finished her senior year at the school.

Amazingly, Jenny planned, in only seven weeks, an absolutely gorgeous wedding to be held at Hampton Park Baptist Church. I drove home for the 1992 New Year's holiday (two days off), and that was the last I saw Jenny until our rehearsal dinner. I feverishly focused on MCES and getting ahead with my academic load, since my wife soon would need my time, too. Plus, this physical separation helped us to honor our desire to remain sexually pure and avoid any temptation—(*Hey, we're almost married. It's okay.*)—before we got married.

On Valentine's Day evening we made our vows to each other in front of about 500 friends and family. Jenny looked radiant in her gorgeous full length, hand tailored, white wedding dress and with her hair braided in the back; I wore the same Marine uniform worn the day we got engaged.

Several cadets I knew traveled from The Citadel to arch swords at our wedding. As we prepared to leave for our honeymoon, we found my GMC Jimmy filled with pink balloons and decorated with phrases written on the windows with white shoe polish. I took out my Marine officer's sword and popped enough balloons so that Jenny and I could sit in the front seats. Driving away, we heard quiet laughter and discovered Jenny's youngest sister, Emily, hiding under a mountain of balloons in the back seat. Since *three's a crowd,* I stopped, ordered eleven-year-old Emily out and popped the remainder of the balloons to see if there were any other stowaways. Our decorating committee roared with laughter as Emily climbed out of my SUV.

We honeymooned in Asheville, North Carolina, at the Grove Park Inn and caused a stir when we walked into the lobby on a Friday night: Jenny still in her wedding dress and me in uniform. We visited the Biltmore House in Asheville on Sunday. On Monday morning, wishing that we could have had a longer honeymoon, Jenny and I returned to South Carolina, and in the afternoon, I returned to Courthouse Bay.

Each weekend after that, I drove to South Carolina, and we enjoyed a weekend marriage. Recognizing that we had very little time together as a married couple, we were still on our best behavior—at least I was *trying* to be. We put our differences aside and focused on seeing the best in each other, thinking the best of each other, and cutting each other lots of slack. In my mind, I had this marriage thing figured out—it was *dating with marital privileges*.

In the meantime, I requested a modification to my orders: for an accompanied tour on Okinawa, and the Marine Corps was more than glad to approve that request. The Corps saved significant costs in my going accompanied to Okinawa for a 36-month tour instead of sending one lieutenant to/from Okinawa for a 12-month tour followed by his/her replacement for 12-months, followed by a third lieutenant.

During her spring break in April, Jenny flew to Camp Lejeune to attend my graduation from MCES Combat Engineer Officer Basic Course; then we drove to Edisto Island, South Carolina, for Honeymoon: Part Two. One evening, while getting ready for bed, Jenny said, "I have something to tell you."

Long pause.

Brushing my teeth, I looked up, saw her reflected image in the mirror, and asked, "What is it, Sweetheart?"

Another long pause.

"I'm pregnant," she said.

I nearly swallowed my toothbrush! Jenny being pregnant was the furthest thing from my mind. She told me our baby was a *honeymoon baby*.

We decided to wait to announce our news to the community, besides our families, until Jenny arrived on Okinawa. While we were thrilled with the news that we had a baby on the way, we were overwhelmed. Jenny's friends and family had just weeks earlier thrown her a bridal shower—and Jenny wasn't sure she was ready for a baby shower.

In May, I flew to Okinawa and reported to 3d Combat Engineer Battalion (CEB). Two weeks later, I was re-assigned to 3d Marine Division Adjutant's office as the Division Awards Officer, since 3d CEB had too many lieutenants and my assignment was an accompanied tour. Initially, I was disgruntled at not becoming a platoon commander at 3d CEB—that's what I wanted to do in the Corps. However, in hindsight, this deviation was from God's hand: I learned how to correctly write an award for a deserving Marine and was able to avoid the six-months-is-all-the-time-you-get-to-be-a-platoon-commander cycle because of an excess of lieutenants at 3d CEB.

I completed paperwork to request military family housing and waited for Jenny to finish her student teaching, graduate from BJU and coordinate with Brad and Peg Lapiska's help to obtain a plane ticket from the military transportation office to fly to the *Land of the Rising Sun*. After living apart for over a month, I felt grateful to be with Jenny in our temporary home in Okinawa.

We stayed in the military's temporary accommodations (*The Lodge*) while we waited on our assigned quarters to be cleaned and renovated. One day I arrived home from work and found Jenny crying. I wondered, *What did I do? I've been at work*.

Jenny told me, "I know I'm supposed to be here with you, but I miss my family so much."

I held her, and we talked some more. I wasn't sure what to do.

The next day at work, I spoke with my boss, First Lieutenant Scott Van Zandbergen, and requested his advice for how I could help Jenny. He immediately called his wife Diana and told her which room Jenny was in at The Lodge. Diana drove over and took Jenny to the Van Zandbergen's home at Camp McTureous. Jenny and Diana quickly became best friends. That night when I walked into our tiny room, Jenny was smiling again.

We plugged into the chapel on base at Camp Courtney, and Jenny began attending a weekly ladies' Bible study. I spent four months at the Division Adjutant's office and was then reassigned to 3d CEB as a Platoon Commander. A week later, my 30-plus Marines and I deployed for over a month to Pohang, South Korea, via Air Force C-130s. I felt grateful to be able to make a weekly phone call to Jenny.

Jenny's pregnancy progressed smoothly. In November, she asked me to put together the crib we had purchased. Thus began my certification to be a dad. That night, while Jenny alternately paced the floor and rocked in her new rocking chair, I finally wrestled with *some assembly required*, and—*voilà!*—we had a crib ready. We went to bed around midnight but shortly thereafter, Jenny woke me.

"I think I'm in labor," she said.

We grabbed her bag, and I drove at top speeds, and then some, on the Okinawa expressway—the Japanese version of an interstate—to the U.S. Naval Hospital at Camp Lester. During her labor, I made the mistake of letting Jenny hold my hand during a contraction (instead of giving her a tennis ball that we had brought in her bag) and quickly learned that adrenaline boosts strength, even in my five feet, five inches tall wife. She absolutely crushed my hand.

We welcomed Daniel Franklin White, III (*Lil Danny*) in the afternoon of the next day. Minutes after helping move Jenny and Lil Danny into a recovery room, I broke down crying. Overwhelmed that he wouldn't nurse right away, I worried that our baby wasn't normal.

Jenny, knowing I'd had only one hour of sleep since the previous day, gently comforted me and let me know that Lil Danny would nurse when he was hungry. She and he figured out the mechanics soon thereafter. In November 1992, I received the best present possible: bringing my bride and firstborn home on my birthday.

Jenny was an amazing mother, and I felt grateful for her mother's heart as she cared for our baby, Lil Danny. I tried to figure out what being a father meant. Looking back, I realize that the training to drive my truck far exceeded that for being a father—or a husband.

I learned quickly that the weekend marriage we experienced from February to April was not the norm for married life in Okinawa. After beginning to see each other daily and spending more time together, I realized my wife did things that bugged me. We began having *dynamic discussions* or *intense moments of fellowship* (a.k.a., arguments), and, to my surprise, Jenny let me know that I did things that bugged her. I couldn't believe what she was saying! We sometimes called our respective parents and expressed our viewpoints—each of us hoped to learn how to convince the other that he/she was wrong. Our parents wisely said that we needed to talk with each other. We soon saw the wisdom of this after receiving our first long-distance phone bill of $400 and realizing that the phone company was not a non-profit ministry. That bill made a big dent in that month's second lieutenant paycheck.

One rather memorable event happened just before Christmas. Jenny, who absolutely loved holidays, wanted to decorate our fifth-floor apartment. I, on the other hand, did not. I could have won an Emmy playing the role of Scrooge that year. Feeling down in the dumps that we were halfway around the world and away from family for Christmas, I thought, *Why bother?*

Two of our dear friends, Scott and Diana Van Zandbergen, invited us to their home so we could teach them the Shaw family's Christmas tradition of constructing and decorating gingerbread houses for consumption on New Year's Day. Upon our arrival, Scott and Diana realized that neither Jenny nor I were in the holiday spirit. They helped us talk about what happened earlier in the *Okinawa White House* that afternoon. After a few minutes, I realized how ludicrous my *Why bother?* view had been and what my wife was asking. The next day I bought a Christmas tree, lights, and decorations—and Jenny was smiling again. I later joked with the Van Zandbergen's that they helped save our marriage during its first year.

In January 1993, my platoon and I deployed for two months as part of our combat engineer company to Camp Fuji on mainland Japan. We conducted training with demolitions, various weapons, and land navigation, and then developed a draft minefield breaching SOP (standard operating procedure). Upon returning to Okinawa, my platoon prepared to support Battalion Landing Team 1st Battalion, 5th Marines (BLT 1/5) as part of the 31st Marine Expeditionary Unit (MEU) Special Operations Capable (SOC). We began to complete a host of individual training requirements: annual weapons requalification, swim qualifications (since we were deploying on board U.S. Navy ships), demolitions refresher training, and squad-sized then platoon-sized patrolling techniques. Six-day workweeks became the norm. In May, we chopped over to BLT 1/5 and training increased, often evolving into seven-day workweeks.

In June, Jenny and Lil Danny flew back to South Carolina for my sister's (Jane) wedding and to let our families meet my pride and joy for the first time. After helping Jenny and Lil Danny make their outbound flight from Naha International Airport to Greenville, South Carolina, I cried my eyes out while driving back to our empty home.

During that time, I began to get off track and lacked balance in my life—again. I was strong physically and was taking adequate care of my mental and emotional needs but began to neglect my faith journey.

I began to worry about getting promoted from Second Lieutenant (2ndLt) to First Lieutenant (1stLt). Later in my career, I realized that the qualification to get promoted to 1stLt was *to fog a mirror*—meaning *just be alive*. Therefore, being alive in May 1993 guaranteed that I would be promoted from the gold 2ndLt rank insignia to the silver 1stLt rank insignia. Yet, I was worried about this automatic promotion and how to get a jump on my peers.

I called Brad Lapiska, and we talked for about twenty minutes. I was enthused about the Marine Corps and my accomplishments thus far. Days later, Brad typed me a letter, challenging me about our conversation. His words were to this effect: "Danny, I'm concerned about how you're doing. You only talked about the Marine Corps during our phone call. Never once did you mention how you and Jenny are doing. Are you attending church? What's it like being a father?"

Brad realized I was unbalanced and graciously tried to help me.

To my detriment, I ignored his missive.

In fact, I remember being upset with his questions and thinking, *Of course, I'm going to talk about the Marine Corps. It's a manly organization. I'm doing some great things here on Okinawa as a junior officer and want to be a success—like Brad and other senior officers. I'll just work harder to beat out my peers for promotion.*

So, much of the time that Jenny, our son Lil Danny, and I could have had together—especially when our platoon wasn't in the field training for deployment—I squandered on busywork at the office, so my senior officers would see me hard at work.

A WIDOWER'S WALK

CHAPTER 5

A Growing Family

From July to September 1993, my platoon and I deployed with BLT 1/5 on the USS *Belleau Wood* (LHA-3) to Tinian, Hong Kong, Singapore, and Australia. Deployment on a Navy ship for nearly three months is a world all its own. The ship appeared huge in port, but after we got underway I realized we were a tiny dot on the surface of the vast Pacific Ocean—seeing only water for 360 degrees. When flight operations ended, I went on the flight deck and watched some of the most beautiful sunrises/sunsets of my life. I looked out the helicopter's window every time when returning to the ship from training and wondered in amazement that this seemingly insignificant postage-sized stamp of metal was my temporary home. A couple of times I looked up at the stars and saw a black canvas covered with millions of twinkling diamonds and was reminded of how big the LORD is—and how small we humans are.

From that opportunity of being forward-deployed, I, as the combat engineer expert for the BLT and the MEU, learned invaluable lessons, and grew significantly as a leader of Marines.

My platoon of thirty-eight Marines and one Sailor completed every task professionally and expertly. During our return to Okinawa, I reflected on Brad's challenge and realized he had been correct. It was true—I had been unbalanced and needed to work on my relationship with Jenny. I stopped dating her after we started married life on Okinawa—assuming I knew everything there was to know about her. We had been seeing each other since October 1986, nearly seven years. I determined to set aside money in our budget to pay for childcare for Lil Danny and take Jenny out on dates. I wanted her to know how amazing she was to me and how thankful I was that she had said "Yes" to marrying me.

We pulled into port at White Beach, Okinawa, and offloaded our gear from the ship; we then loaded our platoon and equipment onto trucks and headed back to Camp Hansen, toward the northern end of the island. I was happy beyond words to see my beautiful bride waiting for me at a playground. But Jenny wasn't alone. She was with a little stranger.

Walking up with my loaded sea-bag on my back and rucksack on my chest, I was astonished at how much our infant son, Lil Danny, had grown! My memory of him was based on photos taken when he was four months old. Jenny gave me those photos to take on deployment. Now, he was eleven months old—and toddling around. Lil Danny returned the favor. He looked up at me and seemingly said, *Who are you?!? And why are you getting in the car with Mama and me? I don't know you!* Fortunately, after some hours of playing with him at home, he began to remember this *stranger* in his life.

A couple of weeks later, in October, we chopped back to 3d CEB. I turned over my platoon to another lieutenant and assumed our company's executive officer (second in command) duties. In late 1993, Jenny announced again, "I'm pregnant." For the second time we chose not to find out the gender of our baby but wait to be surprised.

In January 1994, our company again deployed to Camp Fuji for two months of training and engineer projects, to help Marines stationed permanently there. We were able to coordinate Jenny and Lil Danny's catching a Space-A (space available) flight on a U.S. Air Force aircraft from Kadena Air Base on Okinawa to Yokota Air Base on mainland Japan. I met them at Yokota, and we took the train to Tokyo to stay at the military's New Sanno Hotel for a long weekend. We celebrated our second anniversary together, not apart like the first one. Seeing Lil Danny experience snow for the first time—and seeing the look of wonderment on his little face—became a treasured memory for me from those few days together. It seemed to make the rest of the deployment apart more bearable.

Just over two months after that deployment, I was reassigned as 3d CEB's training officer and then subsequently became the battalion's assistant operations officer. With the exception of a two-week deployment to Chin-hae and Pusan, South Korea, and a few battalion-level field exercises, I was at home every night.

In June, Jenny announced, "I think I'm in labor."

After I called my boss to let him know the news, we gathered Jenny's bag and dropped off Lil Danny with some friends. I talked with them for a few minutes to catch up and see how they were doing. I thought, *Hey, this labor thing is going to be another ten to twelve hours like the first one. We have plenty of time.* Jenny came up to me and said rather firmly, "We need to go to the hospital. Now!"

She wasn't kidding. Just over an hour after checking Jenny in, Hannah Elizabeth was born at the same hospital as Lil Danny. So much for my assumptions about the duration of Jenny's second labor! Hannah started nursing almost immediately—and I didn't lose it like I did with Lil Danny's birth. I will always remember Lil Danny, during his first visit, holding Hannah and having a look of curiosity and love for his baby sister.

One evening, after putting Lil Danny and Hannah to bed, Jenny asked me, "Have you thought about what we would do for our children if both of us died at the same time? Who would we want to take care of them?"

I was repulsed by such a morbid idea of Jenny dying and said, "No, I haven't. Nor do I want to. I don't think that both of us will die at the same time. Besides, we have plenty of life insurance on me as a Marine, along with a last will and testament. I'll be the first one to die." Looking back, I recognize that as an unwise and immature decision on my part.

In December 1994, I assumed the duties of the company commander for Headquarters and Service Company, 3d CEB. Another mentor, Marine Lieutenant Colonel Tyler Ryberg (Marine AH-1 Cobra pilot and Brad Lapiska's friend) took time out of his busy life as a squadron commander to advise and counsel me about the responsibilities of command. In fact, months earlier he had demonstrated what *right* looks like as a Christian Marine officer during his own change of command ceremony when he assumed command of Marine Wing Headquarters Squadron 1. Trying to do the same, I let my light shine at my own change of command ceremony. Several fellow believers, including Jenny, were grateful that I got it right on that occasion. The challenges of company command for 155 Marines and Sailors rewarded me professionally and personally. Shortly after 3d CEB deactivated in April 1995, we left Okinawa.

In May 1995, we executed permanent change of station (PCS) orders to the Marine Corps Mountain Warfare Training Center (MCMWTC) in Bridgeport, California. I served as the Facilities Maintenance Officer / Engineer Officer for the MCMWTC, leading 34 Marines and civilians to maintain $42 million of infrastructure.

A GROWING FAMILY

Bridgeport is high desert, and the MCMWTC base camp sits at 6,500 feet above sea level. By climbing the mountains in the training areas up to 12,000 feet, I could see into Yosemite National Park: absolutely gorgeous scenery, year round—day or night.

I began to get off track, again—slowly turning back to my workaholic ways. Many days, I spent long hours on busywork, in an attempt to be noticed by more senior officers at the training center. With my duties completed, I should have been at home, playing basketball with Lil Danny or helping Hannah learn to ride her tricycle. In 1996, Jenny announced, "I'm pregnant," and we calculated a due date of March 1997.

During Christmas of 1996, a huge snowstorm deposited three feet of snow where we lived in the training center's military housing in Coleville, California. We were thrilled to have my parents, my brother and his wife, and my maternal aunt fly out to spend a White Christmas with us. Twenty-five miles away, up on the mountain peaks near the training center, twelve feet of snow fell.

About a week after Christmas, the weather warmed. Forecasters said the change was due to a *Pineapple Express* moving from Hawaii to the West Coast. That meant the snowline was moving from 5,000 feet above sea level up to 14,000 feet. The twelve feet of new snow—on top of old snow on the mountain peaks—began melting quickly, which led to what the military called Operation Western Flood '97. U.S. Route 395 (U.S. 395) between the military housing and the training center traversed 14 miles through the bottom of a beautiful-but-sheer-rock canyon. Floodwaters from the melting snow washed out that road through the canyon. The result for those of us stationed at the MCMWTC was that, instead of a 25-mile (one-way) commute to/from work, we had an 85-mile trip (one-way).

The MCMWTC began running a bus daily, departing 5:00 a.m. from the military housing area. Since U.S. 395 had washed out and the mountain passes of other roads were closed off with new snow, the shortest alternate route to the training center required transiting into Nevada and back into California. At 6:00 p.m. the bus departed the training center to return to housing—a two-and-one-half hour trip each way. For the first few days during this time, I rode back and forth daily but began to tire of arriving home exhausted, kissing my sleeping children, eating supper, talking with Jenny, falling into bed, and starting the process over in six or seven hours. Our logistics officer coordinated sleeping space for those who wanted to live at the training center during the week.

Sadly, I defaulted to the easy route. I rode the bus to work on Monday morning and returned home to Jenny and our children on Wednesday night; then I boarded the bus for the training center Thursday a.m. and trudged home for the weekend on Friday p.m. I failed to see the strain this put on Jenny, who especially suffered from lack of adult conversation. I also failed to see that I was losing touch with our children—choosing to be *deployed in the United States*. But I convinced myself that I was getting a lot of work done in coordinating the engineer effort to return the MCWMTC to being operational, assisting the town of Walker with flood recovery, and planning engineer projects in order to repair miles of destroyed training-area roads. (Marine engineer units would complete those projects during the short construction season at Bridgeport—late spring/summer 1997.)

I felt drained on Saturdays after working such long days at the training center during the week. So I linked up with my friends to go fishing for trout or hunting deer, quail, ducks, and geese—whatever was in season. A few weeks later, Jenny told me that she was at her wits' end with me. From her perspective, I treated her like my mistress, housekeeper, and a nanny for my children. I failed to maintain a relationship with her as my wife. Hearing her frame her feelings this way shook me to my core—and into days of contemplation.

Jenny was right. I had failed to be a loving husband. She carried a full rucksack too as a mother to our son and daughter and with one more on the way. I asked Jenny to forgive me and tell me what could be done to nurture our marriage. She said she wished I would make the sacrifice to come home every night, as she and our children needed me as part of their lives. After listening to her heart as she spoke, I began coming home daily.

We elected for Jenny to have an induced labor so she could give birth to our third baby (call sign was *Dash-3*, per Marine pilot parlance) and I could be there with her at the South Lake Tahoe Hospital. I didn't want to be at the training center, 85 miles away, with no vehicle to get to her if she went into labor, because I had ridden the bus to work. Late one afternoon in March 1997, we were blessed with our third child, Ethan David.

A few weeks later, the construction company working to rebuild the 14-mile stretch of U.S. 395 that was destroyed by the flood allowed the training center bus (but no personal vehicles) to navigate through the canyon to and from work, significantly shortening my commute time. I'll never forget how grateful Jenny was. (She had been struggling to nurse Ethan; her body wasn't making enough milk. It pained her to have her baby diagnosed as failure to thrive and have to start giving him formula from a bottle.) She could finally count on a set time each day when I would arrive home in the evening to eat supper, offer emotional support, and physically help her with all three children.

In June 1997 we flew to South Carolina for vacation time with the Whites and Shaws. We drove one Sunday to North Carolina to attend a small church. The morning message was about obeying God. I'll always remember going forward during that Sunday evening altar call; the LORD spoke to my heart, saying, *You need to get serious about serving Me*. I realized He meant for me to quit hiding my light as a Christian and stop acting one way at work, another way at home, and another way at church. He also meant for me to stop being a workaholic. I felt sad to realize that my children had had a *missing in action* father who didn't know them very well. As my relationship with God strengthened, I stopped working as much and came home on schedule. Lil Danny had an amazing knack for shooting hoops with his basketball and throwing a baseball; Hannah loved for me to read to her and push her on her tricycle; and Ethan wanted me to hold him or tickle him. Trying to achieve balance in my life began paying dividends in our home life, as our children quickly demonstrated they had forgiven their dad and really enjoyed seeing me.

In July 1997, Jenny announced, "I'm pregnant," and *Dash-4* was inbound. Jenny and I were in shock at the news of that surprise baby. I received orders to leave the MCMWTC and attend career-level school, which was a nice checkmark for my military resume. As Christmastime 1997 approached, we were in the process of executing PCS orders to attend the U.S. Army Engineer Officer Advanced Course (EOAC) 2-98 at Fort Leonard Wood (FLW), Missouri. After a moving company packed up our entire household goods (minus some clothing), we loaded several suitcases, along with Christmas gifts for our families, into our tan 1994 Ford Explorer, which Jenny drove. I led our convoy in my GMC Jimmy.

A GROWING FAMILY

On Saturday, December 13, 1997, we drove U.S. 395 from Bridgeport to I-40 East to a hotel in Needles, California. Lil Danny, Hannah, and I played in the hotel pool while Jenny did laundry. We ordered pizza before having devotions. We then slept, anticipating another long day of driving.

We planned to spend four days traveling to Missouri, check in at the Marine Corps Detachment at FLW, get a house on post, coordinate delivery of our household goods shipment, and head to South Carolina for Christmas with both of our families before returning to FLW in early January. During a phone conversation with her mom, Jenny said, "I'll be home for Christmas this year."

A WIDOWER'S WALK

CHAPTER 6

The Day Life Changed

Deciding to stop in Kingman, Arizona, for breakfast, we were packed and ready to ride just after 8:00 a.m. Mountain Standard Time on Sunday, December 14.

As I buckled Lil Danny into the Explorer, he asked, "Daddy, can I ride with you?"

I told him, "Buddy, you rode with me for most of yesterday. Go ahead and ride with Mommy until we stop for breakfast; then you can ride with me. You can talk to me on the walkie-talkie that Mommy and I are using to stay in contact."

Lil Danny, five years old, and Ethan, nine months old, rode in the Explorer with Jenny, who was five months pregnant with our fourth child. Hannah, three years old, rode with me.

As we moved onto the interstate (I-40 East), I, in the lead vehicle, asked Jenny if she was OK with traveling the speed limit of seventy miles per hour.

"Yes, but no faster," she said.

I asked Jenny to set the cruise control on the Explorer and watched her in my rearview mirror to calibrate my right foot, and we moved out smartly. We talked about how well our first day (the day before) of traveling had gone, the scenery we were seeing, and that we were getting a good start on the day. We passed beautiful and desolate terrain, and I remember thinking that it would be an awful place to have an accident—there was nothing around that lonely area.

Lil Danny asked Jenny to use her walkie-talkie, and I asked him, "What do you want to eat for breakfast, Buddy?"

He eagerly confirmed his usual reply of "Pancakes!" I told him that it was only about twenty more minutes before we stopped.

About ten minutes later I looked down to see 8:56 on my truck's clock. I then glanced in my rearview mirror and was horrified to see Jenny's vehicle go off the road onto the right shoulder, come back onto the road and begin flipping like a corkscrew approximately four times until it came to rest upright in the median of I-40 East, facing northeast. Slamming on my brakes and steering to the shoulder, I felt my chest tighten and my heart began pounding. I thought, *Oh LORD! I hope it was only a bad accident and the vehicle is only banged up.*

Unsure of where the next exit was, where I could turn around and return to the scene via I-40 West, I raced back, westbound along the shoulder of I-40 East toward my wife and children. I quickly realized there was no eastbound traffic; it seemed as if there weren't any vehicles traveling that Sunday morning. I pulled into the median and told Hannah to stay in my truck. I sprinted to the Explorer toward the passenger side, which was closer to me. The front roof and windshield were partially crushed and nearly every window had been smashed out.

Strapped in his toddler's car seat, Ethan screamed and cried at the top of his lungs. I pulled him out, and he began to calm down. I couldn't see anything wrong with him except faint bruising on his forehead. With the Explorer's windshield and roof caved in like a *V*, I couldn't see Jenny. I called out "Jenny! Jenny!" —but heard no response. Carrying Ethan, I ran around to the driver's side.

THE DAY LIFE CHANGED

Looking through the smashed driver's door window, I saw only the left side of Jenny's face. Her eyes were closed. Her seatbelt held her body upright. I watched her chest for a few seconds to see if she was breathing, but didn't see any movement. I looked for signs of trauma on Jenny's body but didn't see anything. I reached through the window and touched her neck for a pulse. After a few seconds, I was thunderstruck to realize I felt nothing. It seemed surreal as my mind registered this and then slowly realized *Jenny's dead!* With an intensity that seemed primal, looking up I screamed, "No!"

My squared-away world crashed down in shattered pieces. I panicked as reality hit: *Our unborn baby is going to die too!* As a Marine, I had been trained for many scenarios but felt totally helpless in that situation. I knew that Jenny was dead and our unborn baby (five months in utero) was dying—and there was nothing I could do. I cried out in anguish in my heart to God, *LORD, please help me. I can't handle this!*

I desperately looked for Lil Danny, but couldn't find him in the vehicle. I scanned the interstate for him and prayed, *LORD, please don't let the Explorer have rolled over him.*

Traffic on I-40 East began backing up, due to debris from the accident. Almost everything we had packed was strewn for yards along both travel lanes of the interstate. I wondered, *Where are the highway patrolmen and ambulances? Why isn't anyone here to help us? Why is it taking them so long to get here?* A truck driver let me use his cell phone, while he and another trucker held Ethan and entertained Hannah, who was picking wild flowers in the median.

Trying to connect with someone for help, I called my dad and told him there had been a bad accident with Jenny and Lil Danny. I told him, "Daddy, I'll call you back once I know more." Standing in that median near mile marker 31.9 miles of I-40 East outside Kingman, Arizona, I felt alone and forsaken by God.

(I've learned I can't trust my feelings. The LORD made a promise in Hebrews 13:5 [NKJV]: "For He Himself has said, 'I will never leave you nor forsake you.' " In the days afterwards, I replayed the events of December 14 and the aftermath and saw that God had been walking with me—just as He promised. I hadn't been alone.)

Another observation at the accident scene: Death is a real *being*. My senses were on full alert, and I sensed death in a tangible way standing in that median of I-40 East.

One of the two investigating highway patrolmen and an off-duty nurse found Lil Danny about 30 feet east of the vehicle: he was in the median, lying on his back. They began to revive him. I stood over Lil Danny in order to block the sun from his eyes and watched him struggle to breathe. I prayed with tears streaming down my cheeks, *LORD, please help my son. Please let him be okay*. Two ambulances and a life-flight helicopter arrived, and I felt some relief that Jenny and Lil Danny might be okay, that possibly I had not correctly felt Jenny's pulse.

After examining Ethan, the emergency medical technicians were concerned with the bruising on his forehead and face; they felt he might have internal injuries. They recommended that he, Hannah, and I ride in an ambulance to the emergency room in Kingman for further examinations. I helped Hannah into the ambulance, and she gave me a couple of the small, yellow wildflowers she had picked. I placed them in my leather jacket pocket and carried them for weeks.

Still holding Ethan, I started to step into the ambulance, then paused to ask the patrolman who had been working with Lil Danny, "Sir, is my wife dead?"

He looked kindly at me and said, "Yes, Sir. I'm sorry she is. But I've never lost a child in an accident, and we won't lose your son."

"Sir, what will happen to my wife's body?" I asked. "Will she be taken to the hospital?"

"No, Sir," he said. "The coroner will come to the accident scene and take your wife's body in for an autopsy."

I hung on to that patrolman's statement about not losing my son Lil Danny during what seemed like an eternity as we rode in the ambulance to a hospital in Kingman, Arizona. My mind seemed to be spinning out of control, trying to calculate what to do next after realizing Jenny and our unborn baby were dead. Doctors took x-rays and checked Ethan to make sure he was OK, and two kind ladies from the hospital's Crisis Intervention Program watched Hannah and Ethan while I made phone calls to Fort Leonard Wood and Bridgeport. I tried to reach the Shaws to tell them that Jenny had died, but they hadn't returned from church. The hospital graciously paid for those calls.

My phone calls were interrupted and my heart dropped when I looked up and saw the expression on the face of the doctor who had been working with Lil Danny.

"Sir, I'm sorry," she said. "We lost your son."[3]

My shattered world totally disintegrated as she said, "If you want to, you can go in and see him."

I'll never forget how I felt like a drowning man while pushing open the double doors of that ER room and seeing my little boy's lifeless body lying on a stainless steel table. While holding him to my chest, I sobbed brokenly and unashamedly and prayed in desperation, *LORD, I need Your help to make it through this. Jenny's dead and not here to help me. Please help me!*

---

3   According to Lil Danny's death certificate, he died at the accident scene. The Arizona highway patrolman who said, "I've never lost a child in an accident, and we won't lose your son" may not have known Lil Danny had died, or Lil Danny may have died minutes later. The man was trying to give me hope.

After holding Lil Danny's body for several minutes, until my sobbing subsided, I left the room to phone my family and the Shaws, Fort Leonard Wood, Bridgeport, and some friends. I had to tell them that both Jenny and Lil Danny had died. Waves of loneliness and helplessness washed over me. I asked my parents in South Carolina to please fly to Arizona to help me.

I dreaded telling the Shaws about Jenny and Lil Danny. I phoned their home and heard the happy sounds of Sunday lunch taking place as Jenny's sister Anne answered. With as much emotional control as possible, I asked Anne if Mr. Shaw was available, and she then handed her dad the phone. He was very quiet and accepted the bomb blast of tragedy I dropped on him. He amazed me with his question, "How are you doing, Danny?"

I told him, "I'm broken and don't know what to do."

Mr. Shaw told me that the Shaw family would be praying for me and to let them know if I needed anything.

Hannah, Ethan, and I prepared to leave the hospital and check into a Kingman hotel. I dreaded leaving the hospital—perhaps it had become comforting and familiar amid the chaos. The two ladies from Crisis Intervention drove Hannah, Ethan, and me to the hotel.

CHAPTER 7

It's NOT a Platitude…Positive Leadership Makes a Difference

Several friends, family members and Marines called me that afternoon, as I sat in that Kingman hotel room. One call I'll never forget came from the Commandant of the Marine Corps (CMC), General Charles C. Krulak, a four-star general. That conversation is seared into my memory and went something like this:

(Phone rings.) "Hello, this is Captain White. May I help you?"

"Do you know who this is?"

"Yes, sir. You're the Commandant of the Marine Corps." (I recognized his voice, having heard him speak in videos shown at the Marine Corps Birthday Ball ceremonies.)

"I'm <u>very</u> sorry for what's happened in your life today. My wife and I are Christians, and we're praying for you. You are going to have needs that we can help you with. Please let us know if you need anything, since we're not mind readers. Will you promise me that?"

"Yes sir, I will."

"And, Captain White, take as long as you need to make your decisions."

We talked perhaps a minute more and said goodbye.

I sat there for a moment, awestruck! How did the Commandant get my number? And the Commandant had called me—because he was a Christian and a Marine! This was the equivalent of the CEO of a 175,000-person organization calling a hurting employee going through adversity to see how he was doing.

Looking back, even though it was only a three- to four-minute phone conversation, that call threw me a lifeline of hope. A picture—I wasn't alone. Yet, I can't imagine what was on General Krulak's schedule that day as the Commandant. Being responsible for the training and equipping of 175,000 Marines is not an easy assignment on any day of the week. He took time for me and put action into his leadership—not just talking in theory about leadership as the Commandant of the Marine Corps.

As time passed, I replayed that phone call over and over in my mind and realized anew that *leadership does make a difference*—a statement many think is just a platitude. But it wasn't a platitude as I sat—hurting, shaken, and unsure of what to do—with my children in that Kingman hotel room. And that day, my life changed. I began to intently study leadership and keenly observe the now-over-300 leaders I've served with, instead of occasionally remembering Brad Lapiska's advice from May 1991: to pay attention to every leader I served with.

But that phone call was only the beginning of General Krulak's leadership in action. I didn't have a clue as to what we were going to need. However, as I began to realize our needs, the General and his staff (Headquarters, Marine Corps) began providing much-needed assistance. The Marine Corps re-routed my household goods from Missouri to South Carolina, so I could get clothing for Hannah and Ethan—practically all their clothing in the Explorer had been destroyed. The Marine Corps reassigned me to the

IT'S NOT A PLATITUDE...POSITIVE LEADERSHIP MAKES A DIFFERENCE

Inspector-Instructor (I-I) staff in Greenville, South Carolina, so we could be with family and assess what to do next. The I-I staff assisted me with the significant amount of paperwork involving medical bills from the accident and in seeking what funding the Marine Corps was allowed to pay for the funerals. And the I-I staff gave a mountain of toys to Hannah and Ethan from their Toys-for-Tots collected for Christmas 1997.

I learned later at my retirement that General Krulak's leadership was far-reaching. John Bishop, a Vietnam-era Marine and friend, who attended the U.S. Naval Academy during the same time that General Krulak attended, heard part of my story at my retirement ceremony. John passed the details to General Krulak and thanked the General for his leadership and the positive impact he had on my life. General Krulak told John that he did remember phoning Captain Danny White and recalled the tragic details of Jenny and Lil Danny's deaths that took place so close to Christmas. John learned that General Krulak had personally contacted dozens of Marines going through adversity. Many remain unaware of General Krulak's leadership and compassion for Marines that he rendered while serving as the Commandant.[4]

---

4 The impact of General Krulak's leadership in phoning me helped another Marine going through tragedy in the mid-2000's. I had briefly shared my story with U.S. Marine Colonel Tom Clark at a Quantico men's retreat. Tom, a friend and fellow Citadel alumnus, served as the senior aide-de-camp for another Commandant. The CMC office was notified of the horrific circumstances of a senior Marine who lost his two-year old son in a tragic accident. Tom went to the Commandant and asked him to consider calling the Marine. The Commandant declined to insert himself in such an adverse situation. The next day, Tom asked the Commandant again to consider calling that Marine, and he shared that a previous Commandant had contacted a Marine that Tom knew after a tragedy, and it changed that Marine's life. The Commandant considered the request again and made the call. Tom was glad to have heard my story in order to reference it when suggesting that a Commandant bolster another hurting Marine.

During that afternoon after the accident, Brad Lapiska called our hotel room. As we talked, he gave me an invaluable piece of advice based on his experiences in the Corps.

"Danny, get into the book of Psalms each morning," he said. "Read until you find the one verse you can hang on to, to get through that day. Also, keep a journal, so you can look back on this time."

To this day, reviewing the journal that I kept strengthens my faith journey. God gave me a verse each day for what I was facing or going to face during the days after the accident: unpacking boxes to get clothing for Hannah and Ethan and seeing Jenny's clothing and Lil Danny's toys, selecting coffins, intensely missing Jenny on our anniversary (February 14, 1998), and so on. There were days I didn't see how I would make it through the next hour, let alone the next day. I realized that we only get one day at a time from God—or only one marble at a time. Also, I found this amazing: my relationship with the LORD went to a deeper level than I had ever experienced and didn't know was available.

Sadly, before the accident, my sister did not have a clue as to whether I was walking with the LORD or not. She had seen my life and knew I had become unbalanced. I heard later that after my sister learned about Jenny and Lil Danny's deaths, she told friends, "Danny is either going to run from God or run to God. I hope it's the latter."

CHAPTER 8

Pictures of Community

Minutes after the accident that claimed my wife, son, and unborn child, I began learning an invaluable lesson: I need a community. Early in my career, I had a *Lone Ranger* mentality. If anything happened, I consulted with Jenny, we made a decision, and solved the issue on our own. I didn't want to accept assistance from others. Yet in those moments after realizing that Jenny, our unborn baby, and Lil Danny had died, I was humbled to realize my need for help. I could not make it on my own. And God began to give me pictures of a community that would help me. I just needed to ask.

While I was checking into that Kingman hotel, the Rev. Raymond D. Burrows, the pastor of Faith Temple Church located near my parents' home, called the front desk and prayed with me. I had never met Pastor Burrows; he told me that my brother Jon and Jon's wife, Ann, called him with news of the accident. (Jon and Ann had started attending Faith Temple in August 1997.)

Another lady from Crisis Intervention drove to the salvage yard to sort through our destroyed suitcases and clothing and find things worth saving; she brought them to the hotel. The Crisis Intervention ladies helped watch my children at the hotel room while I went through the salvageable items. I broke down crying again after seeing blood flecks on numerous file folders and smelling hydraulic fluid—a smell that permeated almost everything. I weeded out irreparable items and filled a large suitcase that had been almost destroyed in the accident, then placed the suitcase in the hotel's dumpster.

One of the highway patrolmen drove my GMC Jimmy from the accident scene to the hotel to save a towing charge. He told me that after seeing the accident scene and preparing the accident report, he didn't know how I was going to make it, until he started driving my truck and heard a children's Christian song-tape playing in my vehicle.

Knowing it wasn't Firestone tires that had led to other Explorer wrecks (we had replaced the tires in 1996), I asked the highway patrolman if he knew what had caused the accident. The patrolman said that it appeared from the skid marks that Jenny had gone off the road, onto the shoulder, and then overcorrected to steer back into the travel lane. That caused the Explorer to begin flipping.

During that afternoon, two ministers from local churches in Kingman stopped by to pray with us.

I did not want the ladies from Crisis Intervention to leave because I dreaded being alone with only Hannah and Ethan, but they had to get back to their families. Around 4:00 p.m., after I'd ordered supper for Hannah and fed Ethan a bottle, we sat by ourselves in the room. Ethan looked up at me, as I fed him, with total trust in his blue eyes—eyes so like Jenny's. I felt shattered and helpless and just knew Hannah was going to ask, "Where are Mommy and Danny?"—which she did.

I began to cry and brokenly told her that they were in Heaven; she cried streams of tears as I held her in my arms. After a few minutes we walked outside. Hannah looked up into the night sky with her blue eyes, also so much like Jenny's, and said, "Mommy and Danny are up there, aren't they?" Oh, the faith of a little child!

PICTURES OF COMMUNITY

 I stroked Hannah's almost-white blond hair and Ethan's blond curls as they drifted off to sleep in one of the beds. After placing sleeping Ethan into a port-a-crib, I lay in the other bed and wondered what life was going to be like without Jenny, my sweetheart and best friend. I couldn't believe we had started the day together but now she was in eternity, a week before her twenty-seventh birthday. What a loss of an extraordinary lady—a young woman who was beautiful, both inside and out. I was unsure of how to function without her, as our lives had been intertwining more and more since October 1986. Time after time, I replayed the events of that day in my mind: watching the Explorer flipping, checking Jenny's pulse, and holding Lil Danny's body for the last time. My parents arrived at the hotel around 2:30 a.m. (Monday, December 15), and we cried and talked. After a few hours of fitful sleep, my parents took care of meals for Hannah and Ethan, while I called the funeral home, my insurance company, family, and friends. I had no appetite.

 Another picture of God's hand being with me in this desert experience struck my mind while I prepared yet another bottle for Ethan in that Kingman hotel room: if Jenny had been able to nurse Ethan after his birth, then her death would have been even more traumatic for him. I wondered if he would have refused to take a bottle of formula from me in the hours after Jenny died.

 After mailing most of our salvageable items to South Carolina on Monday, we prepared to fly to South Carolina from Las Vegas, Nevada, on a red-eye flight. I left my truck at the Marine Corps I-I Staff parking lot in Las Vegas for safekeeping, until I could return and drive it to South Carolina. Walking through the airport, I wanted the world to stop because mine seemingly had. Seeing Christmas trees and ornaments, I thought about how much Jenny loved Christmas.

Unable to sleep on the plane, I reflected on Christmas memories with Jenny and remembered that if Jesus had not come, Jenny and Lil Danny and our unborn baby would not be in Heaven. Having numbed emotionally until we landed in South Carolina, I walked off the jetway, holding Hannah's hand and carrying Ethan. My brother and sister and their families and Jenny's parents and her four younger sisters stood in the terminal. We all broke down and cried.

On Tuesday afternoon (December 16) I met with the funeral director and began trying to develop an order of service for Jenny and Lil Danny's funeral. I felt very low—like I was sinking slowly in quicksand. Afterwards I visited my paternal Uncle Jim and his family. At that time, my father's youngest brother, Jim, served as the business manager for Holmes Bible College in Greenville, S.C. Uncle Jim's wife Janice had died of cancer in 1990. He shared his lessons learned: look to the LORD and not inward to myself. He would walk with me through this desert. God had a future for me. My sister Jane later mentioned that she saw a big difference in me after Uncle Jim talked with me—I still grieved but was no longer in a despondent depression.

During the few days that passed between the accident and the funeral, time seemed to slow down. We planned the funeral so that it didn't fall on Jenny's birthday, her parents' anniversary, or Christmas. I had to guess at the songs and program Jenny would have wanted for her funeral. How I wish I had not stopped our discussion in Okinawa about what we would do if one of us died.

I was crushed to realize that the funeral bills were nearly $20,000—and Jenny and Lil Danny were not covered with life insurance. I had life insurance policies for only me, since, by my calculations, I would die in training or combat and precede Jenny in death.

The first bill, owed from the $20,000 total, was for grave plots: $6,000 for two graves and perpetual care at a cemetery in Greenville, South Carolina. Some members of Jenny's family wanted me to have her and Lil Danny buried at that cemetery. I began to panic, knowing that there was only enough money in our savings account to purchase one plot.

Pastor Raymond D. Burrows had contacted me on Tuesday afternoon, the day I returned to South Carolina from Arizona. He told me that the Faith Temple church board had agreed to offer me two grave plots in the church's cemetery. I questioned him about this kind offer, since I was not a church member, and he only knew me as Jon White's brother. He graciously pressed the offer, stating that it was a gift to help me, if I needed it. The next day, after considering the two options, I accepted Faith Temple's generous gift.

I later asked Pastor Burrows why he would help me since he didn't know me. I could have been the most foul, reprobate man out there. Pastor Burrows' response impressed me: "Brother Danny, if we can't help hurting people, then we might as well close our doors." I saw his strength of character and tremendous leadership at Faith Temple and remain grateful to this day.

During that week, one of Jenny's sisters, Anne, gave me the verse from Jeremiah 29:11 (CJB): "'For I know what plans I have in mind for you,' says *Adonai,* 'plans for well-being, not for bad things; so that you can have hope and a future.'" I hung onto that verse during the days leading up to the combined funeral services. I couldn't see plans that would prosper me and not harm me; I didn't feel as though a future was even possible. Yet God had made a promise, and I clung to Him and that verse.

I'll never forget how humbling it was to see friends gather around our two families. Almost 1,300 attended the funeral home on Thursday evening when our families received friends. Some people stood in line in the cold for more than four hours. I felt like I had to fight my way through the crowds just to get into the mortuary to view Jenny and Lil Danny's bodies. I looked at their bodies, lying in their coffins, and wept brokenly. I noticed that Jenny's left hand was covered with a crocheted-style glove. (Her left hand had been injured in the accident, but I hadn't noticed that injury when I looked for trauma to her body. Days before the funeral, I requested her rings, and, due to her hand injury, the mortician had to cut her diamond ring and wedding band to remove them.) My heart broke again as I observed that her gloved, left-hand ring finger was bare. The finality of the thought that she had kept her vows to me—*until death parted us*—felt like another dagger to my heart.

Standing at the head of Jenny's coffin, I saw that the morticians had attempted plastic reconstruction to disguise traumatic injuries to the right side of her face—the side of her face I never saw at the accident scene. I thanked God that at the accident I didn't see her severe injuries and have that as the final image of her in my mind. And I thanked Him for the realization that Jenny's body lying in the coffin didn't look like Jenny. My head and heart accepted that she was in Heaven, having completed her *race*.[5] I walked over to Lil Danny's casket and was alone. I saw the bruising and battering on Lil Danny's face that showed underneath heavy makeup the mortician had applied. Lil Danny looked different than when I held his body in the emergency room. I placed his blue-and-white teddy bear and a football in his coffin. I couldn't believe my namesake was dead—and his race was over at age five.

---

[5] "Finishing one's race" refers to a letter that, just before his own death, the Apostle Paul wrote to his disciple Timothy (2 Timothy 4:7)

After our families had a private viewing of Jenny and Lil Danny, I decided to close both caskets during the time our families received friends and for the funeral services.

On Friday, close to one thousand people attended the combined funeral service for Jenny and Lil Danny at Hampton Park Baptist Church. That included thirty-two Marines from Washington, California, Missouri, North Carolina, and South Carolina. Another picture of community reminded me that I was not alone.

I felt that the LORD led me to make a few comments at the funeral about Jenny and Lil Danny and about His help in my making it through that week. I said that Jenny was a model of a passage from Proverbs 31:10-12 (NKJV): "Who can find a virtuous wife? For her worth is far above rubies. The heart of her husband safely trusts her, so he will have no lack of gain. She does him good and not evil all the days of her life." Then Proverbs 31:28-29 (ESV) "Her children rise up and call her blessed; her husband also, and he praises her: Many women have done excellently, but you surpass them all."

I continued with referring to Psalm 127:3-5 (CJB): "Children too are a gift from *Adonai*; the fruit of the womb is a reward. The children born when one is young are like arrows in the hand of a warrior. How blessed is the man who has filled his quiver with them; he will not have to be embarrassed when contending with foes at the city gate."

I thanked the LORD for Lil Danny and what a joy he had been to Jenny and me. I said, "I'm envious of Jenny—she knows now whether we were having a boy or a girl." And the audience laughed with me. I closed with an invitation to talk with anyone who wanted to meet Jesus by accepting him as Savior. He had helped me each moment and day since December 14, and I could not imagine trying to make it without His help and comfort.

The Holy Spirit proved faithful in giving me words to say, which God used to touch the hearts of several people, including one of the Marines who told me how profoundly my brief words had impacted him.

Another picture of community included my seeing how the LORD took care of getting my truck back to South Carolina. Jesse Isbell (a retired Marine working as a civil servant at Bridgeport) and Rick Woienski (then-U.S. Navy chaplain for our Protestant services at the MCMWTC) left California and traveled to Nevada to get my truck and drive it cross-country to attend the funerals. They saved me from having to travel and return to the vicinity of the accident before making a lonely drive back to South Carolina.

Several days after the funeral, I remember feeling alone and forsaken, even though my parents were with me and helped me care for Hannah and Ethan. With Christmas quickly approaching, all the people who had surrounded me seemingly left to go back to living their lives and preparing for the holidays. December 24th was a very tough day. I wasn't suicidal but was tired of the pain and of trying to be strong for Hannah and Ethan. I remember thinking, *LORD, please just take me. I can't take it anymore. I'm tired of trying to be strong for Hannah and Ethan. Would You please take Hannah, Ethan, and me to Heaven, so we can have Christmas with Jenny and Lil Danny?*

While lying beside Hannah and Ethan while they napped, I heard the phone ring and my mom answer it. I heard Mama's footsteps come down the hall; she eased the door open and whispered, "Danny, it's Nancy Spencer. Are you up for talking with her?"

Jenny and I met Nancy and Wayne Spencer in California and became instant friends. I told Mama, "Yes, I'll talk to Nancy." I followed Mama to the den, picked up the phone and said, "Hello, this is Danny."

"I don't know why I'm supposed to call you, Danny," Nancy said. "I feel like the Holy Spirit told me to stop my housework and give you a call. We want you to know that we love you and are praying for you. And God has not left you alone at this time."

I was too choked up and crying to say much during our conversation. Years of military training forced me to put on a *tough guy* image. As a Marine, I believed I was invincible and tears showed weakness. However when reality hits, I've learned that real men do cry…and cry hard.

Later, I thanked Nancy for obeying the LORD, for she had thrown me another figurative lifeline of hope just when I needed it. I will never forget how much her phone call meant in reassuring me that God had not forgotten about me, nor had His people.

A WIDOWER'S WALK

CHAPTER 9

Freedom in Finances

Throughout my adult life I had paid my tithes (ten percent), regularly, to my church at each duty station but had not been generous with the other ninety percent of my income. I focused on my family (a little) and me (a lot) with what was left and had not recognized that all of it was the LORD's—He had just entrusted it to me to steward. I rarely ever gave an offering in addition to my tithe. I was in a figurative prison: *stinginess with my money*.

In mid-January, after helping coordinate the generous gift of two grave plots, Pastor Burrows asked me to speak at Faith Temple.

"Brother Danny, I can preach about God's faithfulness from the Bible—Paul wrote twice[6] in I Corinthians that 'God is faithful,'" he said. "But you're experiencing it right now. A saying[7] I really like is 'He that has an experience is not at the mercy of a man who merely has an argument.' Would you please share what you're learning?"

Having spoken only a handful of times in chapel or church services, I felt nervous but agreed to speak on January 11.

To prepare to speak, I turned to a gift, from Brad Lapiska and Tyler Ryberg, given after Jenny and Lil Danny's funerals—a copy of Jerry Bridges' book *Trusting God: Even When Life Hurts*.

---

6   I Corinthians 1:9 and 10:13
7   Attributed to Thomas Myerscough

Bridges' book enabled me to ground myself with a solid base in the theology of suffering. I realized that God was trustworthy in this desert experience, even though I didn't understand *why* it all happened. *Trusting God* formed the basis of what I learned about the LORD's faithfulness and what I would share at Faith Temple.

The Friday before I was scheduled to speak, my maternal grandfather gave me a $100 bill and said, "Son, I want to help you. I know how expensive funerals can be after your *Mima* [his wife] died in 1989."

My grandfather is not a wealthy man; I appreciated his generous gift, for the balance for the two headstones was due the following week.

On the Sunday I was scheduled to speak in the evening service at Faith Temple, I sat in the 10:45 a.m. service. Right before the offering, I took a $20 bill from my wallet, placed it in a contribution envelope, and sealed the envelope. I felt pleased to be giving more than just my tithe.

In a quiet, gentle way during the offering prayer, the LORD spoke to my heart, saying, *Give Me the $100 bill.*

In my mind I said, *No way, LORD! I have to pay off the balance for the grave headstones next week. With that big bill to pay, I need that $100 bill—and a lot more. Tell You what, LORD. I'll give You a second $20.*

I took out another envelope, placed both $20 bills inside and sealed it. I felt very impressed with my generosity and negotiation skills with God.

Again the LORD spoke: *Give Me the $100 bill.* It seemed so real that I looked around to see if someone behind me was talking during the offertory prayer. No one was behind me.

Feeling completely foolish, I took out a third envelope and placed the $100 bill inside. Placing the two $20 bills back in my wallet, I said, *LORD, I feel like a complete nut! I hope that that was You speaking to me. I don't know how I'm going to pay the bill that's due next week.*

That evening I shared what God was teaching me during that desert experience with the adversity I was facing. Afterwards, Pastor Burrows said he felt the LORD leading him to take up an offering to help me. There was a small group attending that Sunday evening service, and I assumed the offering would be an honorarium and might replace the $100 I gave that morning.

After the service, I scurried in the dark through the rain to my GMC Jimmy and, once inside, turned on the dome light and opened the envelope, which contained a check. Seeing the amount, I began to sob brokenly. The church's offering was enough—almost to the penny—to pay off the balance for the headstones! I wasn't alone in the desert I was passing through. I could trust the LORD to provide.

Another learning point involved seeing friends associated with The Citadel (my alma mater) organize and contribute to an account that provided funds to help me with funeral bills. God was living up to one of His names: *Jehovah-jireh* meaning *The LORD who provides*.

And that wasn't the last learning point in my process of being freed from bondage to money. Colonel Ahearn, the Chief of Staff at Marine Forces Reserve, contacted me in March 1998, just as he had done almost weekly, to see how I was doing. During that March phone call, we exchanged general information, and he asked me if I had any financial issues. He didn't accept my nebulous answers and asked point-blank, "Do you have the financial means to pay for the funerals?"

I swallowed my pride and admitted, "No, Sir. I do not." He specifically asked the amount owed, and I told him.

Within two weeks, he told me to ask the I-I staff for a set of orders to fly to Washington, D.C., to meet with Major General Thomas Wilkerson. After Colonel Ahearn picked me up at Reagan National Airport, we went to lunch and then drove to Headquarters Marine Corps at the Navy Annex. I met General Wilkerson, and he presented me with a check from the Marine Corps Law Enforcement Foundation and another check from the Fisher House Foundation. Through Colonel Ahearn making some generous people aware of my situation, the funeral bills were paid in full!

On the return flight to South Carolina, I felt almost as if I didn't need the plane to fly back. I was ecstatic beyond words to see God being *Semper Fidelis* ("Always Faithful") in providing for me when I could do nothing. Having seen the LORD repeatedly take care of my two small children and me increased my faith to trust Him with all my finances and to be ready to give as He prompted, in order to help others who might need assistance in the future.

Later I discovered Dave Ramsey's insights about how to handle money from a biblical perspective. As Ramsey teaches, we shouldn't spend money and go into debt to impress people we often don't know or don't like. Rather avoid debt and live on less than you earn to save and give to help others. This paradigm enabled many generous people to assist me with paying for the funeral expenses.

Additionally, I learned from the Rev. Robert Morris, author of *The Blessed Life,* some of the most biblically based teaching I've ever read (or seen on YouTube videos) about how the LORD views money and His guidance on managing the funds He sends our way. God is extravagantly generous toward us, and He wants us to be generous too.

CHAPTER 10

Stay Marine?

Two weeks after the combined funeral service, Brad Lapiska and Tyler Ryberg flew to South Carolina to meet with me concerning whether I could stay in the Marine Corps or not. As a combat engineer officer, I had to be worldwide deployable yet was now a single parent. I expected to get my thank-you-for-serving pink slip and be told that my service was no longer needed. My MOS as a combat engineer and being a single-parent seemed incompatible.

After talking to the head of the officer assignments branch at Headquarters, Marine Corps (with whom I had served in Okinawa), Brad and Tyler told me, much to my surprise, that I could stay in the Marine Corps—and that if my duty station request was at all reasonable, I could choose my next assignment. This was amazing because, typically, the Corps picks your next assignment and you salute smartly and say, "Yes, sir!" while heading out the door.

I didn't know whether to stay in the Corps or where to go if I did stay in. So I prayed, *LORD, please let it click in my spirit when I get to the place You want me to be.* Even today I'm not sure what my definition of *click* meant, yet God knew my heart and how to answer my prayers.

I decided to visit Fort Leonard Wood, Missouri; Quantico, Virginia; and Camp Lejeune, North Carolina. My logic was that if I remained in the Corps and needed to deploy, my parents could quickly arrive to care for Hannah and Ethan. Those duty stations wouldn't be too far from my parents' home—as compared with a West Coast or an overseas assignment. If things didn't click at one of those three places, I was going to take it that God wanted me to resign my commission and get out. The idea of leaving the Marines seemed intimidating, since the military was all I had known since high school—yet Jenny had been by my side since 1991.

In January 1998, I flew to Missouri to visit Fort Leonard Wood (FLW) and spoke with the Marine Detachment leadership. The agreement included that if I selected FLW then I would attend the EOAC as a student and upon graduation would become a team leader/small group instructor as well as the Marine representative for the EOAC. Practically this meant Hannah, Ethan and I would not move for over three years—which had a lot of appeal for my children's stability.

I was amazed at the close-knit chapel community and the strong presence of God at a weekly Friday night praise-and-worship service. I wrote that day in my journal: *Very promising out here in Missouri.*

After that service, I met U.S. Army Chaplain Tom Solhjem and shared with him my story of God's help to that point. After a momentary pause, he said he felt the LORD leading him to ask me to share during the Sunday morning service at Soldier Memorial Chapel. He felt my story would encourage and boost the faith of his congregation that had been praying for me since the accident. I didn't feel prepared, but I agreed to speak.

On Saturday I spent time with God and felt a quickening in my spirit, but wasn't sure if FLW should be my next duty station. Had I found the *click* place? I wrote in my journal: *Have been wondering, talking to God today [and asking] if FLW is the place we should come to.*

On Sunday morning, a U.S. Army chaplain candidate and his wife sang several songs and spoke for the majority of the service. Tom then introduced me, and, with fear and trembling, I shared my heart for a few minutes with approximately two hundred people. I thanked them profusely for their prayers for my children and me, and told them about how God had been walking daily with me since the accident and about what I was learning. In closing, I challenged them to live each day as if it might be their last and to live each day as if it might be their loved ones' last day. Tom gave an altar call and a young lady accepted Christ. I was amazed that the LORD was touching lives with my story. Afterwards Tom told me that he'd never seen God move in a service at FLW like He did in that one.

After the service, Lieutenant Colonel Harv Nelson, the FLW Marine Detachment Commanding Officer, invited me for a meal with his family and others. I felt grateful to meet those fellow believers and learn about their lives. As Carolyn Henderson, an Army chaplain's wife, and I talked, we discovered that we both hailed from the same area of South Carolina.

In February 1998, seemingly out of the blue, Carolyn called me in South Carolina and graciously offered to provide full-time childcare for Hannah and Ethan, if I selected FLW as my next assignment. She said she would be glad to take care of them in her home or mine. I was overwhelmed at God's provision that was available at FLW.

Also in February, I drove with Hannah and Ethan to Fredericksburg, Virginia, to stay with the Van Zandbergens, our family friends from Okinawa, while visiting Quantico. I met several kind people who offered help if we moved to Quantico. I ate meals with numerous Marine friends stationed in the Northern

Virginia (NOVA) area and requested that they pray for me about decisions I had to make.

After lying down to sleep on the evening of Valentine's Day, I wept with silent, gut wrenching sobs until my pillow was soaked. I missed Jenny so intently that my crying caused my core muscles to ache the next morning—the day after what would have been our sixth anniversary.

I thanked God for the opportunity to meet with Brad Lapiska and Tyler Ryberg in NOVA and receive a shower of encouragement from them that seemed to flow from Heaven. Brad asked me to share my story at his church, Engleside Baptist Church, on Sunday at its 8:30 a.m. and 11:00 a.m. services. *So was Quantico the "click"?* I wondered.

Toward the end of February, I traveled with Hannah and Ethan in my GMC Jimmy to visit Camp Lejeune. Denny Phillips, who was Nancy Spencer's sister, graciously offered to watch Hannah and Ethan during the day. I visited various options for serving at the Marine Corps Engineer School (MCES) or Facilities Maintenance at Camp Lejeune.

With so many friends in the Marine Corps at Camp Lejeune and since that location was the closest of the three bases to my family, I wanted to go to Camp Lejeune. Plus Jenny and I had dreamed about getting stationed there in order to be closer to both of our families.

Driving back to South Carolina on Saturday, February 28, 1998, I thought over the Camp Lejeune option. Taking their naps, Hannah and Ethan were sound asleep in the back seat of my truck, and I had turned off the radio to avoid disturbing them. Alone with my thoughts, I heard only the hum of my truck's engine and its tires on the road. I mused about Camp Lejeune, Quantico, and FLW, and whether I had felt a *click* at any of them. *I get to pick my next duty station! I can do a lot of good at Camp Lejeune at either MCES or Facilities Maintenance. I'm eager to be closer to South Carolina. Also, I know that many others want me to select Camp Lejeune if I continue serving in the Corps*, I thought.

What seemed like an audible voice spoke to me. I knew the Holy Spirit was zeroing in on my heart as he asked, *Are you going to please Me? Or others? I've shown you where to go.*

Instantly I knew what He meant. I asked for His forgiveness for trying to convince myself that Camp Lejeune would be better instead of FLW. I prayed for His help and made my choice: FLW.

The next week, I called the Marine in charge of captain assignments (a.k.a. *the monitor*) and requested orders to FLW. He asked me if I was sure about the timing, since he was willing to schedule me for the July 1998 EOAC class (EOAC 4-98). The monitor's offer was amazing as I'd done nothing for the U.S. taxpayers for almost four months. Each week I called the I-I staff to check in for accountability and visited periodically to complete military health insurance paperwork or finalize travel claims. For a split second I mulled over the July option and considered obeying God by going to FLW—but waiting until July. I definitely enjoyed eating my mom's cooking, being near my parents and siblings as well as Jenny's family, and experiencing a real sense of community in South Carolina.

I told the monitor, "Eric, I've prayed about it and don't know why, but I need to attend the April 1998 class of EOAC. I'm nervous about FLW, as it's the furthest duty station from my parents and siblings. And it's a U.S. Army post. Yet I know God is leading me there."

The monitor accepted my reasoning and issued orders authorizing me to repack our household goods, ship them to Missouri, and report to FLW in time to begin EOAC 3-98 on April 20, 1998.

Faith Temple Church performed a dramatic production in early March, and I helped my brother construct the stage and took a role in the production. After the second and final performance, I spoke with Pastor Burrows.

"Pastor Burrows, I feel the LORD has led me to stay in the Marine Corps," I said. "I've decided to report to FLW for the April class of the Army's EOAC. After graduating from the EOAC, I'll continue serving at FLW as the Marine representative to the EOAC."

He replied, "I'm grateful, Brother Danny, for God leading you to this point. I know He will continue directing your steps."

"Sir, I have submitted to the LORD that if He wants me to remarry, I will do so," I said. "I asked Him to make it crystal clear to prevent me from making an emotional decision and hurting Hannah and Ethan. If God does lead me to remarry, I'll never meet my wife in Missouri. During my visit to FLW in January, I didn't notice any single ladies—even though I wasn't looking. I'll likely meet a lady here in South Carolina when we come back to visit."

"Brother Danny," Pastor Burrows replied. "We've been through some tough times together, with the pain in your life after your wife and son and unborn baby died in December. In faith, I believe God is going to help us rejoice together in the not-too-distant future."

Later in March, a pastor in Savannah, Georgia, called out of the blue and asked me about sharing my story with his church. (This pastor was a friend of Tom Solhjem.) I had told God that if I were ever asked to speak, I would take it that He had opened that door and He wanted me to share, so I accepted the pastor's invitation.

En route to Savannah, I stayed overnight with a friend in Charleston, South Carolina. I had made an appointment to meet with Major General John S. Grinalds, U.S. Marine Corps (Retired), who, at the time, served as the president of The Citadel. General Grinalds had

Childhood years (1972)
Back (L to R): Mama and Daddy
Front: Jane, me, and Jonathan

Two of my best friends
L to R: Jon, Jane, and me
(Unless otherwise noted, photos by author)

Last Parade as a Citadel cadet (1991)
L to R: Kelly Young and me

Weekend Jenny and I were engaged (1991)

Family photo after Okinawa tour (1995)
Back (L to R): Me and Jenny
Front: Lil Danny and Hannah

Ethan's dedication at the MCMWTC, Bridgeport, CA (1997)
Back (L to R): Jenny and me holding Ethan
Front: Hannah and Lil Danny

Last family photo (1997)
Back (L to R): Hannah held by me
Front: Lil Danny and Jenny holding Ethan

Wrecked 1994 Ford Explorer

Wrecked 1994 Ford Explorer

How I defined myself = a "human doing"

Funeral service at Hampton Park Baptist Church
Danny's casket (white) and Jenny's casket (brown)
(Photo by Mike Osterhoudt:
taken from video of funeral service)

Grave plots donated by Faith Temple Church
(Photo by Ann Burrows)

Sketch by Nora for our wedding invitation

Marriage to Nora at Soldier Memorial Chapel (1998)
L to R: Ethan, me, Hannah, and Nora

Family photo: Lydia's birth (2000)
L to R: Me, Lydia held by Nora, Hannah, and Ethan

Family photo after Okinawa tour and Ian's arrival (2004)
L to R: Ethan, Hannah, Nora holding Ian, me, and Lydia

Family photo after Phillip joined us (2008)
Back (L to R): Ethan and Lydia
Middle: Nora and Hannah
Front: Phillip and Ian

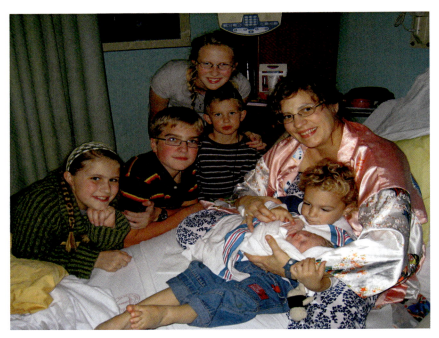

Family photo after Erik's arrival (2009)
Back: Hannah
Front (L to R): Lydia, Ethan, Ian, and Nora holding Phillip holding Erik

Picture of God's grace: two girls and four boys (2011)
Back (L to R): Erik and me
Front: Lydia, Hannah, Nora, Ian, Phillip, and Ethan

Picture of God's overflowing grace:
two girls and five boys (2014)
Back (L to R): Hannah and Ethan
Front: Nora holding Noel, Erik, Lydia, Phillip, me, and Ian
(Photo by Kassi Hillhouse
www.kassihillhousephotography.com)

Family photo after Christine's arrival (2016)
Back (L to R): Ethan, Ian, me with Noel,
Nora holding Christine, Hannah, and Lydia
Front: Erik and Phillip

Family photo after Anders' arrival (2018)
Back (L to R): Lydia, Hannah, Ethan, me holding Christine, and Ian
Front: Phillip, Noel, Nora holding Anders, and Erik

Family photo (2020)
Back (L to R): Ian, Ethan, and me holding Anders
Middle: Erik, Phillip, Nora, Lydia, and Hannah
Front: Christine and Noel

Nora and me

sent me a handwritten note with his condolences and asked me to meet with him if I was ever in the Charleston area. I wore my service "A" uniform and met him in his office. He amazed me with his humility and devotion to God, his family, and his calling. He prayed with me and expressed his gratefulness that I knew the LORD and that He was helping me.

I arrived on Friday in Savannah to speak at the Southside Assembly of God Church's special evening service. Again, after sharing what I was learning in my desert experience, a lady came forward during the altar call to receive Christ. I marveled at seeing God at work again, using my story. After spending some time in prayer and thanking God for another opportunity to share my testimony, I sat and waited for the service to end. A lady sat down beside me and quietly thanked me for sharing. She said she felt the Holy Spirit impressed her to tell me, "Danny, you won't be lonely long. And the LORD has something big in store for you that will blow your mind."

I thanked her for passing along that information but began thinking, *What do you know about my situation? How can you know how long I will be lonely?*

After the pastor and his family and some friends took me out to eat for supper, I checked into my hotel room and continued mulling over the lady's words. As I questioned her *message,* the Holy Spirit spoke to my heart and said *I gave that word for you. Don't belittle it.* I asked God to forgive me but wondered about what *you won't be lonely long* meant. I had not been seeking another wife and assumed I would remain single. I didn't want to hurt Hannah and Ethan by remarrying and then discovering my wife did not love my children—the fairytale evil stepmother syndrome.

Weeks after Jenny's death, I talked with the LORD during a run through the woods on my parents' property. I said, *I'll never remarry.*

It hurts too much, losing Jenny. Anyway, I don't believe anyone will accept me and love Hannah and Ethan.

After the run, as I cooled down with some stretching exercises, the LORD quietly spoke to my heart, saying, *What if I ask you to remarry?*

I considered God's question for a few days, and then answered Him with this thought: *No, LORD. This pain of losing Jenny and Lil Danny is almost unbearable.* I resisted the idea of remarrying, even if God asked me to.

I felt no peace in my life for hours, so I relented and prayed, *LORD, please forgive me. I'll remarry, but only ask that You show me that it's clearly Your leading. I'm willing to remain single and lonely and not see Hannah and Ethan hurt. Please make it clear if and when You want me to remarry. I'm not looking for another wife.* The only problem was I failed to record this milestone in my journal.

April 1, 1998: Movers came to my parents' house and packed up and shipped to FLW all my household goods.

As I prepared to leave South Carolina, I received an e-mail from Carolyn Henderson, the chaplain's wife I met at FLW in January.

"We haven't heard from you, Danny, and assume that you're getting out of the Marine Corps and God is calling you to preach," she said in essence. "Any way my health will not permit me now to take care of your children."

I thought, *Excuse me, LORD. It's been a little rough down here, in case You haven't noticed. I thought we had childcare worked out at FLW. That was one of the reasons I felt like it "clicked" and shaped my decision to go there. I need some smooth sailing now. God, I'm convinced You want me to go to FLW. All my stuff is in a moving truck en route to Missouri, and I have orders to continue serving on active duty. I can't back out of going to FLW. Who's going to help take care of Hannah and Ethan while I go to work? Will I have to leave them with my parents and commute to South Carolina as often as possible?*

But there was no answer.

I replied to the chaplain's wife via e-mail: "Ms. Carolyn, I'm still in the Marine Corps and will be reporting to FLW in a couple of weeks. God will make a way for us and help me find care for Hannah and Ethan. God's going to take care of it."

Until that point I wanted to have all the answers and a plan before stepping out. Yet, I had no plan or answers for how to proceed with childcare and had to totally trust God.

I decided to leave my children with my parents until I could find a house on post, coordinate the delivery and unpacking of our household goods, and set up the house. On April 8, 1998, I broke down crying when hugging Hannah and Ethan goodbye—and they cried too. I drove to Faith Temple, said goodbye to Pastor Burrows, and walked to Jenny and Lil Danny's graves, making a figurative altar before the LORD. I wept brokenly for a long time and poured my heart out to God. I told Him, *LORD, I am going to get in my truck and drive the nearly 800 miles to Missouri. I do not have any answers or ideas or plans. Now I have no childcare for Hannah and Ethan. You are going to have to help me because I can't do it myself. If You don't help, I will fail.*

I continued crying while driving away from what had become familiar and comfortable—and replayed the accident and events of the last four months. Yet, the closer I got to FLW, the more of God's peace flooded my heart.

CHAPTER 11

Easter ~ New Beginnings

The next day, at Fort Leonard Wood (FLW), I checked in with Lieutenant Colonel Harv Nelson, the Commanding Officer of the FLW Marine Detachment, and reported for duty. He invited me to the chapel congregation's dramatic production of Ruth Elaine Schram's Easter play, *The Living Last Supper*, to be held on Thursday and Friday evenings at Soldier Memorial Chapel. Having nothing else to do, I attended both presentations and felt tremendously blessed by the author's insights.

On Friday evening I walked out of the sanctuary and ran into Mrs. Judy Carlson. I remembered briefly meeting her in January after the FLW chapel service where I shared my testimony; I thought I remembered she was a chaplain's wife.

"Danny White!" she exclaimed. "I knew I recognized that tall frame and smile from somewhere. We weren't sure where you would end up, or when you might arrive if you chose Fort Leonard Wood."

"Thank you," I said. "I'm glad to be here and will be happy to get my home set up so Hannah and Ethan can join me. My parents are watching them for me right now."

"Did you enjoy *The Living Last Supper?*" she asked.

"Yes, I did," I said.

I looked behind Judy and saw a beautiful young lady. Her long brown hair framed her face in soft curls. I noticed a gentle, doe-like look in her eyes. Judy gestured in the young lady's direction and said, "This is my daughter, Nora. She helped with the make-up for *The Living Last Supper.*"

Nora and I shook hands and smiled at each other but didn't say much. I walked to my truck. I didn't give this meeting a second thought. What I didn't know was how Nora felt when she saw (in her words) "a tall, handsome-looking man with an easy smile" walk through the chapel's double doors. Nora thought she knew all the young men from chapel—all married or just soldiers passing through. She later told me that when she heard the name *Danny White,* time seemed to freeze in that moment. She thought, *You mean the older, grieving widower whose children I had offered to watch? He doesn't seem so much older, now!*

I drove from the chapel to Chaplain Tom Solhjem's home off post. Since my social calendar was very open, I eagerly accepted Tom and his wife Jill's invitation to spend the evening with them. While unsure who brought up the childcare issue, I told them about Carolyn's e-mail and my need for help. Tom and Jill said they would let the chapel community know about my need. I returned to my Bachelor Officer Quarters (BOQ) room feeling relieved that someone in the chapel might be able to help me care for Hannah and Ethan.

The next Sunday (April 12) was Easter. I attended the morning service in Soldier Memorial Chapel and sat by myself on the left side of the chapel and wondered what was going to happen to me at FLW. This thought came to me: *What was it like for the disciples on that first Easter morning?* As I reflected on that question, it hit me that their world had been shattered on Passover. The disciples had seen their Rabbi Jesus crucified and buried—they had not seen Jesus overthrow Rome and free Israel as they had expected. None of Jesus' followers, except for the few people whom the angels had told, knew their Rabbi had risen from the grave. They had only word-of-mouth (or maybe *donkey express*) to pass the message—instead of the instant-communication methods available 2,000 years later.

In mere milliseconds after those thoughts, the LORD began to put back together the pieces of my shattered world. As the sun streamed through the chapel windows like a spotlight shining from Heaven, I glanced up and saw, walking up the right aisle and into that spotlight, the same beautiful young lady I'd met on Friday night. She wore a lovely yellow dress. (For the life of me, I couldn't remember her name.) I sensed the Holy Spirit speaking to my spirit: *There's your next wife.* Those words seemed so real and audible that I whirled around to see if what I had *heard* was from a human being who was trying to play a cruel trick. No one was seated within twenty feet of me. Then the Spirit spoke to me again: *There's your next wife.* (God knows... I'm slow.)

I felt as if my entire world went into a tailspin—the same as when an airplane goes out of control and begins spinning around as it falls. I thought I had lost my mind because considering marrying this young lady was too soon. In America, there is an unwritten rule that you have to mourn a year after the passing of a spouse. I was confused; in my mind I still was married to Jenny—in fact, I was still wearing my wedding band from Jenny. I didn't want to let other ladies know I was now available. I felt as if I were being unfaithful to Jenny in looking at another lady as a possible wife. And I had prayed during the previous four months and asked the LORD to keep me from rushing into marriage and possibly hurting Hannah and Ethan by making a hurried or emotional choice. In spite of the loneliness of being a widower, I didn't want to marry someone who might not love my children. By my calculations, I would remain single.

I don't remember much about the songs we sang or what the chaplain said in his message. The tailspin didn't subside. I began thinking, *Uh, LORD, I* think *it was You who said that lovely young lady will be my next wife. How am I going to meet her—and tell her this "divine" news? The odds are very high that she will not welcome a pick-up line of "Hi, I'm Captain Danny White, and God said you're going to be my next wife! Kachow, Baby." If I try that, she's likely to slap me!*

After the chapel service, Marine Lieutenant Colonel Harv Nelson invited me to his home (located on post) for Easter dinner with his family. Upon walking in, I was absolutely floored to see *my next wife*—Elnora Lee *(Nora)* Carlson—and her family at the Nelsons' home. I didn't know that Nora and her family were good friends with the Nelsons. (Nora's dad, U.S. Army Chaplain Tim Carlson, served as the FLW Deputy Post Chaplain [second highest-ranking chaplain at FLW].)

During the meal, I sat at one end of the table, and Nora sat to my immediate left. As one can imagine, the tailspin intensified at this point, although neither the Nelsons nor the Carlsons were aware of my unease. As I tried to keep my yellow paisley tie out of my mashed potatoes and attempted to appear suave and debonair, I kept thinking, *Wow, my next wife! She's beautiful! This can't be happening. I can't remarry so quickly. What will people think?*

After the meal, all of us gathered in the living room to talk. Nora excused herself to go upstairs to take a nap. (She'd had a poor night's sleep with curlers in her hair—in order to create her amazing look.) As soon as it seemed polite for a Southern gentleman to depart, I thanked the Nelsons for their gracious hospitality, said goodbye to both families, and returned to my room at the

EASTER~NEW BEGINNINGS

BOQ. I couldn't handle the way Easter had gone! Nora woke up and found that *Captain White* had departed. As the Carlsons and the Nelsons played a game of cards, the Nelsons teased her, saying, "Nora, you chased away a potential card partner by your absence."

On Monday, I continued checking in at the Marine Detachment and started looking for a house on post for Hannah, Ethan, and me. That afternoon the phone rang in my BOQ room:

"Hello, this is Captain White. May I help you?"

"Hi, Danny, this is Chaplain Tim Carlson. We enjoyed eating Easter dinner with you. How are you today?"

"I'm doing well, Sir; thank you. How are you? It's good to hear from you."

"Danny, I wanted to let you know that we've heard you might need help with childcare. Nora is looking for work. She would like to help take care of Hannah and Ethan if you need assistance."

(At that point, I felt like my tailspin went completely out of control.)

"Sir, thank you for passing along the information about Nora's offer. I'll consider it and look at my academic schedule. If it looks like we could work out the hours, I'll follow up with you or Nora."

I quickly hung up the phone and went to my knees in prayer. I asked God, <u>LORD, what in the world is going on</u>?

No answer, so I went for a long run.

I wrestled with feeling attracted to Nora, while knowing that if she took care of my little ones, she would be in my home—and that would be awkward. I wrestled and prayed again and again during the week. The Bible records that Jacob wrestled with God for a night.[8] I tried to do so from Monday to Friday. Toward the work

---

8   Genesis 32:22-32

week's end, I felt like an emotional wreck. What I didn't know is what was going on in Nora's life and mind.

God had Nora in a *holding pattern* in Missouri. After teaching second grade for a year in Alaska, she felt God closing that door, and she returned to Missouri. She decided to take time off—up to a year—from teaching or attending school to work on personal goals and enjoy her family. She planned to return to school in the fall of 1998 to earn an art degree, as God had worked through circumstances to block her earlier attempts. She was looking for meaningful work but no job seemed worth the long commute. She wondered what God's purpose was for her in *Fort Lost-in-the-Woods*—the name soldiers gave to Fort Leonard Wood, Missouri.

Nora felt as though she didn't fit in. There was a major shortage of young singles in her community. Most of her friends at Protestant Women of the Chapel (PWOC) were military wives with children. For some time, she had been in a relationship that held significance for her, but finally realized it was headed nowhere. "Imagine my delight," Nora later described, "when I discovered God had brought me not just another guy, but a real *man* in my life."

I proceeded to get into a lather about Nora being my next wife and her offer to care for Hannah and Ethan. I again called my Uncle Jim, and asked for advice. Uncle Jim was ecstatic for me and advised, "Danny, you're not wired to be a father and a mother to Hannah and Ethan. I'm grateful to God for bringing Nora into your life. The biggest compliment you can pay Jenny is to remarry quickly, as it shows that you valued your marriage to Jenny and that she meant the world to you—and you're not doing well alone without her. Don't worry about waiting a year to remarry—it's not prescribed in the Bible. I searched the Bible diligently after Janice died. Waiting a year is a societal norm."

On Friday evening I attended the chapel's weekly praise-and-worship service. During prayer time, I went to the altar and poured my heart out to God: *LORD, I give up. I can't take it anymore—my being in a figurative knot, wrestling with whether or not to accept Nora's offer to care for Hannah and Ethan. I don't even know my academic schedule yet. Will it work for Nora to take care of my children? You have guided my steps since Jenny and Lil Danny and our unborn baby died. You led me to FLW, so I will continue trusting You, LORD. You love Hannah and Ethan more than I do. If it's Your will for Nora to watch Hannah and Ethan for me while I'm in the EOAC, please work out the hours so that she can keep them. And <u>please</u> calm my anxieties and help me be certain that I'm in step with You on this issue."*

I truly believe that if I had recorded in my journal my earlier request to God—to make it clear if He wanted me to remarry after a run on my parents' property—then I wouldn't have been in such a tailspin.

As I left the service, a peace settled over me, and on Sunday, I accepted Nora's offer to help care for Hannah and Ethan after they arrived at FLW. We agreed that we would work out the hours for childcare based on my academic schedule.

(I later learned that Nora previously had offered to help care for Hannah and Ethan after hearing me share my story during the January 1998 Soldier Memorial Chapel service. She mentioned her childcare offer to Lieutenant Colonel Harv Nelson, but he didn't feel led to pass along her offer. So I had no idea she had made such an offer. Thus, she felt rejected when I never contacted her about caring for my children. As months passed, Nora became disenchanted with the idea of working for a man who lacked the courtesy to decline or accept her offer of childcare. When the Solhjems passed along my need for childcare to the chapel congregation, Nora heard the news via her parents. Chaplain and Mrs. Carlson challenged Nora to consider making again the offer to help *Captain White*. God softened Nora's heart toward me, and, despite her initial reaction to protect her heart from another rejection, she agreed to let her dad pass along her offer to me—she felt *she* couldn't personally make that offer again.)

I asked Nora if we could talk after the morning service on Sunday. I reviewed her handwritten resume she provided and accepted her offer. We discussed weekly payment and her plans to carpool to FLW with her dad. I asked her if she would mind if I called her to discuss the power of attorney that we both thought would be a good idea—in order for her to provide care for Hannah and Ethan with any medical emergencies. I wanted to tell her about my children. And I wanted to get know this amazing lady that God had pointed out to me.

Nora kindly gave me permission to call her. We talked about the power of attorney and information I needed from her to complete that agreement. By the end of that hour-long conversation, Nora felt convinced that I'd wanted to share information about my children and myself and get a feel for Nora's personality and how she and I would fit in a work-type relationship. However, Nora's parents and siblings didn't agree. Nora was irked by their presumption about the length of our conversation. "He's my <u>employer!</u>" she defended. "And he's a dad who cares about his kids!" The Carlson clan exchanged knowing glances.

But when I called again a night or two later, Nora finally *got a clue*. I began sharing how I had talked with Nora's friends, a married couple, about how nice it was to have someone to talk with (after my loss) who wasn't family. Nora wondered to herself, *Why is he talking to my friends about me?*

I then took the plunge and asked, "Would it be okay if I call you sometimes, not work-related, but just to talk?"

Nora thought, *How can I refuse? He's a grieving man!*

But what a shock for Nora. She was so intent on appearing mature enough to care for my children that she didn't realize she'd convinced me that she, though five years my junior, might also be a suitable companion for me. Nora felt shocked, confused, and flattered all at once: *Captain White's interested in me?!* (She thought I was practically a celebrity already at FLW.) When Nora's parents followed her into her room that night after her long phone-conversation with me, she was definitely blushing—and eating humble pie.

April 15, 1998: I moved from my BOQ room to my quarters. That week was more *desert-like* as I received our household goods and began unpacking. I broke down, weeping, after two long days of taking out our belongings by myself and trying to set up furniture, decorations, and photos exactly as Jenny had done with our home in Bridgeport. Perhaps I was attempting to create a sense of comfort from what we had experienced at the MCMWTC. I felt alone and forsaken. Again, my feelings proved untrustworthy.

A FLW family housing inspector had helped me inspect and then sign for and take responsibility for my quarters (home on post). I shared part of my story with him while we walked through my soon-to-be home. He stopped by on April 16 to see how I was doing. I told him, "It's been a tough day." He prayed with me. Another reminder—God hadn't forgotten me.

A short time later, Chaplain Tom Solhjem called, seemingly out of the blue, to see how I was doing.

"Not well," I said. "I'm really missing Jenny and Lil Danny as I try to set up my quarters."

Tom offered to bring over the chapel youth group and ignored my rather weak protests. They showed up, and, while Tom cut my heavily overgrown lawn with his riding mower, those precious young people began to unpack boxes and shove pans into kitchen cabinets and towels into the closet. It was total chaos. But it was exactly what I needed. Tom apologized for what seemed to him the disorder generated by the youths' random attempts at unpacking; he worried that they might have caused me more work. I explained that God had used him and the chapel youth to bless me by letting me know—again—that I wasn't alone. Besides, I told him, "The chapel youth helped unpack a bunch of boxes and free up more space in my quarters. And they enjoyed smashing the empty boxes. I'll gladly tidy up afterwards and sort out the correct locations for the items the youth unpacked."

Nora's youngest sister, thirteen-year-old Anna, was one of the chapel youth who helped in the random unpacking. Anna also served as a spy for Nora by describing *Captain White's* attitude and appearance.

CHAPTER 12

Courting Nora

As Nora and I continued getting to know each other, I asked her, "Will you go out with me on a double date with Nathan and Julie Bond?"—implying "Will you begin a romantic relationship with me?"

She said, "Yes!"

I asked her, "Would you like me to request permission from your parents? That's how I operated with Jenny's parents."

Nora thought about it for a moment. She said, "I am a twenty-three-year-old adult and have taught school thousands of miles away in Alaska. But I do think it would honor my parents for you to ask them." She later mentioned that it meant a lot to her that I had asked to court her before she met Hannah and Ethan. This reassured her that I was interested in her—not just in her *nanny* abilities.

My mom and dad arrived with Hannah and Ethan on April 21 and stayed until May 12 to help them get settled into our new home and establish some sense of normalcy as they transitioned from the Mountain View *White House* to the Fort Leonard Wood *White House*.

April 30, 1998: the Carlsons invited all of us to dinner at their farm. My parents took Hannah and Ethan to *The Farm*[9], and I joined them after my academic day was over.

---

9   The name Nora's family gave to their property.

Not knowing Nora at all, I assumed she would like the cowboy look—since every lady in my limited network liked cowboys. So, I prepared to charm her by changing my fashion statement from Marine camouflage uniform to cowboy duds. From Nora's perspective it was kind of the reverse of Clark-Kent-in-the-phone-booth-becomes-Superman: my Marine uniform was her preferred *Superman* outfit. Unbeknownst to me, Nora was anti-cowboy, based on previous encounters with the type. She later told me she was horrified to see me walk down the stairs dressed in a red plaid flannel shirt tucked into dark blue jeans and wearing classic cowboy boots. I was missing only the hat and spurs—which thankfully were still at my quarters.

That evening, after we left, Mrs. Carlson asked Nora, "He could wear cowboy duds every day for the rest of your life. Are you ready to consider that possibility?" Nora thought maybe her mom should have asked, "Is it the man or the wardrobe?" Nora chose the man. (A couple of weekends later Nora was glad for her decision: she saw me wearing a T-shirt, shorts, and sandals—non-cowboy duds. She realized I had other clothes in my wardrobe.)

We enjoyed a relaxing evening, collectively getting to know the Carlsons and vice-versa. Nora had prepared an incredible meal of chicken potpie, so I was relieved she knew how to cook. Nora's teenaged brothers, Kristian and Nels, bragged on her cooking to no end throughout the meal, as well as recounted her string of admirers. What I didn't understand was that this was Kristian and Nels' way of impressing—not scaring off—*Captain White,* the gentleman caller, who actually met with their approval to pursue Nora.

As we prepared to depart, I wrestled with whether to ask Chaplain and Mrs. Carlson for permission to court Nora, knowing that the next Monday she was going to start taking care of Hannah and Ethan—or asking for permission another time. My parents departed from the Carlson farm to return to FLW with Hannah and Ethan. I stayed behind and asked Chaplain and Mrs. Carlson if I might talk with them. They agreed and we went into their semi-private library.

I told Chaplain and Mrs. Carlson that I would like to court Nora and requested their blessing to do so. Chaplain Carlson said it was important that whoever Nora married must be able to provide for her and take care of her. He felt I had proven my ability to care for a family by having already been a husband and father. He gave me his blessing and permission to court Nora. Unbeknownst to me, Nora stationed her sister Anna in a nearby bedroom to overhear her parents' conversation with me. She had panicked and begged Anna, "I can't listen. You try to listen to what Danny says to Mom and Dad. But don't be seen!" Nora then crept downstairs to the kitchen—to *innocently* wash dishes.

In hindsight, I see that the LORD definitely led me to request Chaplain and Mrs. Carlson's permission to court Nora before she started keeping the children. I don't think I had the wherewithal on my own to think of that. God wanted to deny the devil a foothold that might cause problems for us after we married—Nora might have wondered if I married her just so she would take care of my children.

Nora began taking care of Hannah and Ethan while I attended classes at the EOAC. She rode to FLW with her dad and returned home with him in the evenings. To this day, it is amazing to me how the LORD provided the opportunity for Nora to take care of the children for five months before we were married. He knew that Hannah and Ethan needed bonding time with Nora and stabilization. If I had courted another lady and married her, my children would have had to adjust to that new person.

One afternoon I returned home from school and talked with Nora while waiting for Chaplain Carlson to pick her up. I looked tenderly into her eyes and confessed, "I look forward to the day we no longer have to say goodbye."

We were only two weeks into our relationship, and Nora wasn't prepared to hear those words. She had no ready response, so she quickly sought to change the direction of the conversation without insulting me.

"So . . . you really think we're supposed to be together?" she demurred.

Long pause on my part.

How do I answer Nora's rather pointed question? Should I tell her about Easter or not? I thought. I decided that honesty was the best policy and answered her, "I didn't come to Fort Leonard Wood expecting to meet my next wife. But God pointed you out to me on Easter Sunday morning at the Soldier Memorial Chapel. And He said you would be my next wife. So I'm not just looking for someone to date on Friday evening."

That subtle-as-a-chainsaw response was more unsettling to Nora than my previous statement.

In 1997, God had given Nora a *heads up* about our relationship. She and her family were visiting their old church at Fort Story, Virginia. Two different former parishioners of Chaplain Carlson gave Nora a prophetic message on the same day and independent from each other:

Stacey gave Nora a pendant necklace she'd been carrying in her purse. She'd been waiting for the right pastor's daughter to give it to. Stacey felt that God had a distinct purpose for the one who would receive that gold pendant depicting two cranes. Stacey thought the two cranes with adjoining beaks was a Korean symbol for marriage.

August, a man who heard Nora sing a rare solo *(Road to Zion)* in that chapel service, pulled Nora aside after church to tell her a message that came, he said, not from his words but from God's. That message went like this: *God was preparing a man for Nora. This man was not ready yet, but when the time came (be it two years or two months), it would come fast, like a rollercoaster, and not to fear.* (At the time, Nora was in a relationship that she was certain would become a courtship. Nora couldn't understand why God felt the need to provide such reassurance about a relationship that was going as planned.)

And after Nora and I met, our relationship, to her, seemed to be on a fast rollercoaster ride. In fact, she purchased her wedding dress, a beautiful dress at a steal-of-a-deal price, around two weeks after she met me—and after my not-so-subtle response to her deflection. She said her defense for buying that dress was 1) I had said I never wanted to say goodbye to her and 2) she figured that if I changed my mind, *somebody* would marry her.

I'll always remember Nora's brother Kristian's baccalaureate service on May 13, 1998, at Plato High School. Kristian's class must have been *desperate*, for they asked me to speak. I wore my Marine Corps dress blue uniform with ribbons and marksmanship badges. I started with Luke 2:34 (ESV), a Bible passage telling of the time Simeon blessed Jesus and said, "Behold, this child is appointed for the fall and rising of many..." I asked the students to consider if their lives would cause the rise or falling of many and then shared my story of Jenny, Lil Danny, and our unborn baby's deaths and challenged those precious seniors not to take life for granted. I felt surprise at the warm response from Kristian's class toward a stranger speaking at their baccalaureate, and after leaving the podium, was pleased to see Nora smiling at me.

During the benediction prayer at the baccalaureate service, I reached for Nora's hand for the first time. She reached back. "I think the rollercoaster ride began with fireworks that very moment," Nora recalled. We held hands on the truck ride back to her parents' house. Nora couldn't stop smiling. Already, she felt as though her feet could no longer touch the ground.

Before I began courting Nora, I told Mr. Shaw, Jenny's father, that I had met Nora and planned to date her. I wanted to honor the Shaws and Jenny and not do anything behind their backs. Mr. Shaw thanked me for letting him know that I had met Nora.

Our first *official* date was a double date with Nathan and Julie Bond on May 14, 1998. Nathan was a new friend I met during the EOAC, and Julie was a friend of Nora's from PWOC. Both Nathan and Julie had been plotting to get Nora and me to meet. They didn't know God had been working on that too—since Easter.

The Bonds picked me up in their white Jeep, and then we picked up Nora at one of her friend's house off post. We rode to Applebee's in Rolla, Missouri. I sat in amazement, watching Nora place her order: she wanted two dressings to the side with her salad and an extra plate for her entrée. I had never seen such a thing and wondered if I could put up with that kind of particularity if we got married! How would I handle this beautiful *Princess and the Pea?*

Nora and I spent more time together as my schedule allowed—mainly on the weekends. At one point I told her, "You let me know how often you want to get together: once a week, once a month—or every day!" That line made her smile.

Nora initially was hesitant to be seen together in public, wanting to avoid gossip—she feared that well-meaning romantics would spread the news. She was in a high-profile position as the deputy post chaplain's daughter and perceived me as somewhat of a celebrity—the handsome Marine-gentleman widower on an Army post. Nora's resolve to date secretly was quickly broken at a PWOC couple's dinner that we attended. Nora said she couldn't resist the opportunity to have *such a man* at her side. Besides, the faces around us all wore the smiles and winks of dear friends.

Nora felt apprehensive about marrying a widower and becoming an instant mom. We continued to spend time together and build trust. She moved past the bewildering, disconcerting thought of living out a 1998 version of *The Sound of Music* and warmed to the idea of linking her life with mine. (A good friend cautioned me that Nora might be tempted to marry me because she loved my children. Nora has since teased me that she married me in spite of my children. But the truth is all of us took turns winning her heart.)

Since Jenny and I had had three children and one more on the way, Nora wanted to know if I had undergone surgery to prevent having future children. At first, I was taken aback with her question about such a sensitive topic but then realized Nora wanted to have children of her own too. She was greatly relieved with my somewhat blunt response: "Jenny and I had planned to *take the bullets out of the pistol* but we never followed through with a permanent solution."

On June 9, 1998, I took Chaplain and Mrs. Carlson to lunch and asked their permission to ask Nora to marry me. I thanked God profusely that they said "Yes."

Not yet knowing Nora's tastes, I asked her to accompany me to select her diamond. On June 17, 1998, we visited a jeweler in Rolla, Missouri. Nora credited me with getting her ring *just right*: from the designs etched on the band to a modified princess setting—a setting oriented like a baseball diamond rather than a square. Nora recalled that the jeweler explained that they didn't set diamonds that way. She was impressed that I didn't accept the we've-never-done-that-before response and tactfully pressed the jeweler to at least try to set her diamond that way. He eventually agreed—and Nora had her dream fulfilled, with a custom-made engagement ring.

I selected Saturday, July 18, as *the day*. Nora's parents watched Hannah and Ethan. Nora and I went for a drive in my GMC Jimmy, down a country gravel road: Astoria Drive—a name, Nora thought, that sounded like a storybook fairytale name for a road. We found a quiet spot to pull off the road. I had brought chilled, sparkling grape juice, and two glasses—and her diamond. I poured the juice into the glasses, looked intently at Nora, and handed her the diamond. She thought, *That's it!?! Try again!!*

"You need to get on one knee and ask me," she coached.

Realizing I had blown it, by failing to remember this was Nora's first time to get engaged, I dropped to one knee and asked, "Will you marry me, Nora Lee?"

Nora paused momentarily, then said, "Yes!"

I slipped her diamond onto her left ring finger. I held her hand for a few moments and admired what that ring represented in her life and mine. We kissed and our passion quickly built—and we realized that basing our relationship on the physical was not a solid foundation. Both Nora and I agreed not to kiss again until our wedding day. We wanted to remain sexually pure before we were married, and we realized that unbridled kissing might lead to the next step. Nora asked if we could take a short walk to ponder the huge commitment we had made to each other—which we did.

We drove to another road, one of Nora's favorites for walking, and enjoyed an incredible view of the rolling Ozark hills as we talked about our movement toward matrimony. We returned to The Farm to announce our news to Nora's parents and her four siblings, who were still living at home.

The following day, during Sunday morning chapel service, we announced our engagement. The entire congregation seemed to buzz with the news—the widower was marrying the nanny.

Nora walked the second mile almost daily as she cared for Hannah and Ethan: she prepared supper for us and returned home and helped do the same for her family. One day she went all out and made one of her special dishes: chicken corn chowder. She cooked the meal and had it on the stove as I arrived home from school.

"Please let me know how you like this," she said. "It's one of my signature dishes. Make sure you eat it warm."

I agreed to do so and bid her goodbye. I decided to take Hannah and Ethan to the *Blue Park,* a name we gave a playground that was almost a half-mile walk from our home. For efficiency, I turned the kitchen stove to its lowest setting and put Nora's chicken corn chowder meal on to warm just before we left for the playground. Hannah and Ethan climbed up and down the equipment and played in the sand. I gathered them up and we returned home about 45 minutes later. As we walked in, I smelled a burnt odor. Racing downstairs to the kitchen, I ruefully discovered that Nora's prize dish was ruined. *What do I do?* I thought. Since we were a Marine-family, I dished up the food and strongly encouraged Hannah and Ethan to eat. When we finished eating, the pot was still half filled—enough for the next evening's meal. I cleaned up the kitchen and put the food in the refrigerator.

The next morning, as usual, I zipped to school when Nora arrived. She liked chicken corn chowder so much, and had spent so much time preparing the dish the day prior, she decided to take a bite, cold, for breakfast—and she **never** eats food cold. Nora took one bite and was horrified: *Did I mess it up that badly?* Her next thought: *He burned it! He's so busted!*

I returned home after classes and talked with Nora a few minutes. As we were talking, I pulled out the pot of chicken corn chowder to warm it for supper. Nora instantly pounced on me.

"*What* did you do to my chicken corn chowder?" she asked.

With great fear and trepidation, I admitted my misdeeds of the previous evening. I poured a bowl for Ethan, and he stared at it gloomily. As the steam and the foul odor rose from the bowl, Nora pleaded with me, "Please let me make something else for you all."

I said matter-of-factly, "No, this is fine. We'll eat this chowder."

"Well, then for Hannah and Ethan's sake—please let me make you something else. My dad will be here in ten minutes; I'll make something quick."

I relented and, true to her word, Nora whipped up some leftovers into another delicious meal. And Ethan smiled, in his cute one-year-old way. Chicken with marinara sauce certainly beat burnt soup!

For our wedding invitation, Nora included a poem she composed at age fifteen or sixteen. She recognized that God answered her long-ago wish.

"Whispered Wishes"

If I could see behind the curtains of your eyes,
If I could slip inside your mind for just a day,
If I could only feel the pulsing of your heart,
Then gone my whispered wishes whisked away.

If I could steal into your dreamland unawares,
If I could hear the silent words you softly pray,
Oh, if I could hold your spirit in my hand,
Then gone my whispered wishes whisked away.

If my cheek would dampen every time you cry,
And if you and I could soar into the sky,
And find the land with shooting stars at play,
Then wishes would there ne'er be left to pray.

Elnora Lee Carlson

On Friday, September 11, 1998, we had our evening wedding rehearsal. Nora and I received quite a bit of harassment because we wouldn't kiss during the rehearsal—but we were committed to not kiss again until we were married.

(During the rehearsal, Nora felt that I encouraged her to stick with her dream to face the audience, rather than have her back to congregation . . . just because some said it had never been done. She said, "Danny has, from the beginning, supported my individuality and encouraged me to pursue what matters to me.")

Some members of the FLW chapel congregation were concerned about my marrying Nora and wondered if I was going to treat her correctly. One lady even confronted me after the Friday night praise-and-worship service I attended after the wedding rehearsal.

"Why are you marrying, Nora?" she asked. "You had better not hurt her! If you don't have any good answers, I'm not attending your wedding tomorrow."

I contemplated how to answer that lady and mentally sent a quick prayer up to God to guide me. I told her, "I didn't report to FLW expecting to find a wife. God drew my eyes and heart toward Nora on Easter when He said, *There's your next wife*. I asked Chaplain and Mrs. Carlson for permission to court Nora before she started taking care of Hannah and Ethan. I sought my uncle's advice about remarrying, and he told me I was paying Jenny a huge compliment to not stay single a long time. He said I was essentially saying that marriage had been a blessing for me despite the anguish of losing Jenny. So, I was willing to take the risk and love again. Plus I wasn't a good father *and* mother for Hannah and Ethan."

That lady seemed surprised to hear my explanation, and she accepted it—and I felt glad to see her and her family in the audience the next day.

CHAPTER 13

Marriage to Nora

On Saturday, September 12, 1998, days after my graduation from EOAC 3-98, Nora and I were married at Soldier Memorial Chapel at FLW—the chapel where God had directed my attention to her on Easter. Nora's two brothers, her brother-in-law, my dad and brother, along with Army Captains Nathan Bond and Joe Wyka (friends from the EOAC) were my groomsmen. Nora's sisters, several of her cousins, and one of her best friends were her bridesmaids. Pastor Burrows and Chaplain Carlson officiated the ceremony for us. Even though we took pictures before the ceremony, the image of Nora standing in the vestibule, holding her dad's arm, was forever burned into my memory. Wow! What a heavenly vision! She took my breath away!

Hannah was so sweet on our wedding day. She came up to us at the reception—outside at Nora's parents' farm—wearing a favorite old rag dress (she had changed directly after our wedding because her "beautiful dress" was itchy). Hannah looked up at us with blue eyes and said, "Now I can call you *Mommy* instead of *Miss Nora*." (And yes, I cried).

Nora and I sat at the head table at our reception and listened to guests freely share an assortment of advice, humor, and songs. Like most brides and grooms, we spent almost all our time talking with guests and not eating. I soaked my dress blue uniform with sweat that warm September day and was very glad to shower and change into travel clothes after the reception was over.

Joe Wyka, my neighbor at FLW, kindly agreed to drop off my dress blues at the dry cleaners on post for a much-needed cleaning. My parents drove Hannah and Ethan back to FLW to spend the night at my quarters. The next day they all began their return trip to South Carolina, while Nora and I went on our honeymoon.

I met and talked with several members of Nora's extended family while waiting for Nora to change and finish packing her suitcase. Nora's sisters and female cousins crowded into her room and gave advice—what to take, what to leave behind—and at times they were not in agreement. One of them even *c*ommented to Nora, "Danny is so kind and patient."

We were two hours behind schedule, and I finally said to a Carlson relative, "Please tell Nora it's time to go." We had reservations at a bed-and-breakfast in Rolla, Missouri, an intermediate stop before catching our outbound flight the next day. Nora emerged moments later, and I almost threw out my back stowing her massive suitcase in the rental vehicle. I had rented a car for Nora and me to drive to the St. Louis Lambert International Airport for our outbound flight. Not knowing Nora's brothers or male cousins very well, I kept the rental car locked up tight—since we didn't need any stowaways as Nora and I departed. I expected a caravan of Carlson sons, cousins, and distant relations to attempt to follow us. To prevent such shenanigans, after helping Nora into the car, I peeled out in a cloud of dust, and we were off. I kept an eye out for trail vehicles, but after five miles of driving like one of my biblical heroes, Jehu (he drove his chariot furiously), I didn't see any miscreants following us.

MARRIAGE TO NORA

We felt grateful to find a small basket with snacks and sparkling juice at our bed-and-breakfast room. We both were famished.

I almost died laughing the next day when we were checking in at the airport and saw the tag an airline attendant put on Nora's suitcase; that bright orange tag displayed these words: "Heavy, bend at knees." No wonder I nearly threw out my back lifting her suitcase—it must have weighed ninety pounds. I wished I had interrupted Nora's sisters and female cousins *suitcase packing council* and put a kibosh on bringing the kitchen sink.

After our honeymoon in Australia (I found a steal of a deal), we flew to South Carolina to pick up our children. We returned to FLW where I assumed the duties of a small group leader with EOAC Team "C" of the odd-number cycles (i.e., EOAC 1-99, 3-99 and so forth). I remain grateful for the talented and professional Army engineer officers and international officers at the EOAC whom I taught—and thankful for discovering that God had wired me with the heart of a teacher.

Upon returning to FLW, we said goodbye to Nora's parents, as they were re-assigned to Northern Virginia. I bless God for getting my attention and guiding me to FLW in April to attend EOAC 3-98. If I had waited to attend EOAC 4-98 in late July, which would have been more comfortable for me to do, would Nora and I have even met? I wondered if there had been only two months between my arrival at FLW and her parents moving away if we would have met—let alone married. And if I had gone to Camp Lejeune on my own direction, Nora would not be my wife.

Nora and I had our share of struggles, as most newlyweds discover, about how to budget our money, schedule our home life, and decide which church to attend. But to get a picture of what we also faced as newlyweds: I was a dad who changed a diaper—Ethan's diaper—on his wedding day. We were instant parents with two small children and other issues that arise with a blended family—issues such as: how to deal with three sets of in-laws, how to coordinate time with the Shaws when visiting my family in South Carolina, and how to remember three families' worth of birthdays and anniversaries. The LORD faithfully helped us work through those issues and others. Looking back, I wish I had sought counseling for my marriage with Nora. We had to deal with the aftermath of the accident and our becoming a blended family.

While not doubting the timing of our marriage—my only wish was that I had known the answer to what would later be a life-changing question "Who are you?" I believe in my heart of hearts that we would have had much less friction in the early years of our marriage if I had had a clue about the *baggage* that I brought into our marriage.

CHAPTER 14

Chapter of Life with Nora Begins

Nora wrote the following poems *"Misty Eyes"* for Hannah and *"Heartbreak Eyes"* for Ethan.

"Misty Eyes"

*Where'd you get your
misty eyes?
Are they blue or grey or green
they seem a real surprise,
Oh, where'd you get those
wistful eyes?
Do they hold secrets
from an ancient land?
Only elves, or fairies,
dignitaries understand,
Oh, where'd you get
your misty eyes?
Yeah, where'd you get
those pretty eyes?*

Elnora Lee White

"Heartbreak Eyes"

*Where'd you get your
heartbreak eyes?
Were two specks pulled out of
a pale blue sky?
Were they fringed with black
just to see that some pretty girls cry?
Oh, where'd you get your
dreamy eyes?
Did heaven send them
down on loan?
Was your handsome face
the perfect place to make their home?
Oh, where'd you get your dreamy eyes?
Yeah, where'd you get those
heartbreak eyes?*

Elnora Lee White

    Nora slowly and gently made changes to *my* home on Thayer Street, which I had set up as closely as possible to Jenny's style for our home in California. Nora remembered that I had displayed, on a shelf near the entryway, a wedding photo of Jenny and me. Each day while watching Hannah and Ethan, Nora saw that photo—a daily reminder of what she was about to do by marrying a widower. Nora felt relief to see, days before our wedding, that the photo was gone—a message to her that I was ready to marry her. After we married, Nora made gradual changes to reflect who *we* were as a couple and her new role as the *heart* of our home.

CHAPTER OF LIFE WITH NORA BEGINS

I soon realized that being married to Nora was going to be a lot different than being married to Jenny. My maxim for food: if it wasn't in a plastic bag (as in a military Meal-Ready-to-Eat) and it was at least at room temperature, I was a happy man. One Saturday afternoon, Nora was horrified to see me spoon some food into a bowl and begin eating it. She pleaded for me to let her warm my food in the microwave. I reluctantly agreed to let her nuke my lunch, to keep my new bride happy. A few minutes later, she brought me the food, after she had tasted it and pronounced it *fit for consumption*. I took a bite and immediately couldn't feel my tongue. The food seemed to be the temperature of, well, lava—in fact I couldn't taste much of anything for almost a week. But that food was the perfect temperature per Nora's standard for food temperature. Ah, differences in temperaments and temperatures!

Nora and I talked about having children together and began trying to conceive a child together after Ethan turned two years old. The LORD blessed us with a precious little girl, Lydia Sharon, born in the early hours one morning in April 2000 at the FLW military hospital. She looked so tiny. As she grew, we thought of her as our little elf princess, with pert ponytails and dazzling blue eyes. One day we noticed a fleck of gold in her eyes, which gradually grew until green took over. To us, her birth was the LORD's seal of approval on our family that He put together. As Lydia grew into a beautiful young lady, she evidenced a love for reading and writing and a zest for life.

"Emerald Eyes"

*Where'd you get your
emerald eyes?
Like dew drops sparkling*

on the green, green grass.
Are you a princess trying to
be a peasant lass,
Oh, where'd you get your
emerald eyes?
Where'd you get your
sea-green eyes?
Were you a mermaid tradin'
in her tail?
Did you swim to earth upon
a whale?
Oh, where'd you get your
sea-green eyes?
Yeah, where'd you get
those emerald eyes?

Elnora Lee White

During my three years of instructing at the EOAC, the Holy Spirit opened up doors for me to share with 139 international and U.S. students about God's help in an up close and personal way. Only God could take a tragedy from 1997 and turn it into a testimony of His faithfulness and provision. I lived it and stumbled through it and still remain in awe of how awesome God is.

Some students commented that they were astounded at how I could still be *functioning*—let alone *talking* about my family's tragedy. My response: I made it a day at a time only through a personal relationship with Jesus Christ and with the help of a community of fellow believers. Because of God and His Word, I found—often finding the exact verse to get

CHAPTER OF LIFE WITH NORA BEGINS

through each day—the strength to continue journeying through my desert experience—with the help of a community.

In 2001, my parents and Nora's parents joined us for my promotion to Major(O-4). Then, mere days after 9/11 (September 2001), we packed up our household goods to move to Okinawa, Japan.

(Nora remembers that on 9/11 she was sitting in a waiting room, waiting for her and our three children's immunizations, required for an overseas assignment, when she watched the hospital television and saw the Twin Towers fall. The air felt charged with danger and trauma. She clearly recalls the medical technician shaking his head and clicking his tongue as he scanned the list of required shots. "Hope you survive all these," he muttered under his breath. *Not very comforting!* After we reunited at our home that day, Nora and I wondered out loud if our country would survive. Would we have any family or friends alive to greet us when we returned from our next assignment?)

We arrived on Okinawa, and I checked in with First Marine Aircraft Wing (1st MAW). My orders had changed en route: rather than serving as the 1st MAW Wing Engineer, I reported to Marine Wing Support Squadron 172 (MWSS-172). I served as the Operations Officer and subsequently the Executive Officer of MWSS-172 and learned invaluable lessons about leadership and process-improvement from the three superb leaders who served sequentially as the Commanding Officer of MWSS-172 (Marine Lieutenant Colonels). In mid-2002, MWSS-172 received the Marine Corps Aviation Association's James A. Hatch Award for the best MWSS in the Marine Corps.

During this three-year tour, Nora and I chose to live off base for the entire assignment in Japan. I found that to be a far more enriching way to experience Okinawa than was my 1992-1995 tour when

125

Jenny and I lived on base. We learned where to shop for good deals and outfitted our apartment with some Okinawan furniture that fit Nora's style.

Nora and I faced many weeks apart when MWSS-172 deployed to Tinian, the Philippines, and South Korea. The first deployment was a large exercise on Tinian, a small island located fifty miles (eighty kilometers) north of Guam and about five miles (eight kilometers) southwest of its sister island, Saipan, and approximately 1,400 miles (2,253 kilometers) from Okinawa. While apart from Nora for over two months, God gave me a picture revealing how I had been treating Nora. I was leaving her emotional needs unmet, just as my needs for physical intimacy were not being met while apart from her on deployment. (During those months apart we kept in touch via e-mail—a first for me while being deployed. We joked about turning those e-mails into a novel, or a marriage manual.) Upon returning to Okinawa, I shared my insights with her, and she agreed with my lessons learned. We asked some church friends to babysit our children while I took some vacation time. We went to Ie Shima (pronounced Ee-Ee-Shee-Muh) to the YYY Resort for a second honeymoon, and our relationship began to blossom once again.

"Ie Shima's Song"

The sun's already up! Not yet six o'clock.
Bright morning has begun. Make haste! Wash face ~
Pack tote, be gone.
To find the tune so early sung,
Stranger, can you join the song,
God sings to Ie Shima?

CHAPTER OF LIFE WITH NORA BEGINS

Steps carved from a coral cove wind down,
To green shining waters and soft ocean sounds.
A grandmother gathering seaweed from the rocks,
While hermit crabs scurry and boats swim to dock,
A harmony fit for a calm morning walk,
By the waves of Ie Shima.

Stranger, stroll the island shore.
See the yellow-skinned man who pulls an oar?
The boat dock gives a closer look ~
A man aged like his boat and net,
Directs a tune as fish get wet.
Small ones captured, now set free;
The fisherman's hand bells to the sea,
A symphony heard by God and thee ~
Stranger to Ie Shima.

Pick up your tote, farewell the dock,
Greet a curious pair on their well-worn walk.
A man with a twinkle in his eye,
Bows as he leads his pony by.
Short and stout, both patiently plod,
Making pleasant percussion to each other and God,
Across the sands of Ie Shima.

Follow the man and his pony's track,
Right past a woman not wanting to chat.
All clad in white from her toes to her hat,
With her back to the beach, almond eyes toward the song,

A WIDOWER'S WALK

She sits still as a statue while the music swells on.
Do the waves wash her cares as God christens the dawn ~
That shines on Ie Shima?

Flowers and seashells mark the way,
Where butterflies flit and snowy cranes bathe.
Blue painted wings and feathery strumming;
Harps played o'er the ocean drift off at your coming.
Stranger, did you breathe a prayer ~
To touch those harpists in the air,
Soaring over Ie Shima?

Enticed by cranes and butterflies
Back to the dock to your surprise,
A man and a woman pour buckets of song
Dipped from the ocean and carry them home.
You peek in their tank and see only water,
Have they captured God's song
For Asian sons, Asian daughters ~
This Ie Shima morning?

Stranger, watch the pair drive off.
Once again, shoulder your tote.
Husband awaits and eggs and toast.
But just before your journey home,
Let water soothe where feet have roamed.
Hear tinkling wind chimes, coral play ~
While lapped on shore by emerald waves,
As puffs of clouds in silent song
Make melody beneath God's throne,

CHAPTER OF LIFE WITH NORA BEGINS

O'er looking Ie Shima.
Bright morning musn't pass
Unknown ~
Oh stranger, be His singer!
And calm the rushing
World back home ~
Speak songs of Ie Shima.

Elnora Lee White

We plugged into Neighborhood Assembly of God Church, located off base, and helped with the nursery and taught an adult Sunday school class. As a result, we gained a new family while we were away from our extended families. Two distinct memories are with me from that time: the small group study we participated in as we learned to face life and support each other in community; and serving with some very godly men and working with Royal Rangers by mentoring young boys along their faith journeys.

In August 2003, God blessed us with Ian Daniel who arrived late one morning—during a typhoon. We were safe at the Camp Lester Naval Hospital in Okinawa—the same hospital where Lil Danny and Hannah were born. As a baby, blond-haired Ian seemed to always smile, and he brought many smiles and cheer to those who held him and loved him as he looked at them with his twinkling brown eyes. His athletic skills and sharp mind kept all of us on our toes, as he's our resident prankster.

"Chocolate Eyes"

*A chocolate wink
fun loving and precocious
fixed upon baseball
and all things social,
A searching gaze
tender and hopeful,
Where'd you get your
deep brown eyes?*

*They look like chocolate
pools of ice cream.
When I look at 'em
I'm swimmin' in the
richest dream.
Where'd you get your
deep brown eyes?*

*I think God wanted to
surprise us so
He scooped up your
chocolate eyes.*

Elnora Lee White

We had a unique experience during Christmas 2003. We have a very simple nativity set made up of roughly carved figures—each only an inch or two tall. After putting up our decorations in our Okinawa apartment, we could not find the Baby Jesus in a Manger.

CHAPTER OF LIFE WITH NORA BEGINS

We felt like we tore our home apart—no manger. Days before Christmas, Hannah found it, reminding us of a profound truth.

"Wooden Nativity or Baby's Piece"

Baby lost the Baby Jesus.
Just a tiny wooden Jesus.
Painted stable now can't
please us.
Carve'd figures fail to ease us.
"Help us, Lord, find Baby Jesus!"

Said this prayer with Baby's sister,
called to Baby,
begged and kissed her,
could not say to Mom or Sister,
where the Baby Jesus be.
All that night remained empty,
poor, lonesome nativity!

Come next morning,
Sister prancing,
into living room and dancing.
Found the piece, completes the others.
Found it 'neath her own pink covers.
(Had to tell her Mom and Brother.)
Could it be that Baby sought,
a cozier, a warmer spot,
than the Baby Jesus got?

*Or did our Babe without
intention,
a blundering too sweet
to mention,
By misplacing Baby Jesus
'cause our hearts and eyes
to teach us?
How the world looks
like a stable,
empty figures quite unable
to enjoy a single sleigh bell,
or find this Christmas,
peace.
When missing Baby's piece.*

Elnora Lee White

(Lydia Sharon ended up being the culprit.)

In 2004 we left Okinawa for my next assignment at Manpower & Reserve Affairs, Headquarters, Marine Corps at Quantico, Virginia. During that tour I learned much about the complexities of the manpower process—from recruiting to promoting to retaining the right Marines to meet the Corps' mission. Our section planned for the largest end strength growth the Marine Corps had seen since Vietnam—for operations in Iraq and Afghanistan. Congress annually legislates and funds the Marine Corps *end strength* (i.e., how many Marines are allowed to serve on active duty and in the reserves). I asked my superiors for permission to volunteer to serve in Iraq as an individual augment during this assignment, but they denied my request for such an assignment. Their explanation: my present duties were important, too. The *real* reason I didn't deploy: God had His reasons for keeping me at the home front.

After returning to the U.S., we completed paperwork for Nora to adopt Hannah and Ethan. After seeing how much love she had given them, I knew she was a true mother to them. Yet we wanted to ensure that if I preceded her in death, there would be no issues for her in the aftermath.

In May 2006, we moved out of our on-base quarters at Quantico that were scheduled for demolition and reconstruction. We moved to a newly renovated on-base townhome with four floors—that house was a *stair-climbing machine*. In June 2006, God comforted us as we dealt with a miscarriage. We were grateful for His strength and grace as we grieved the loss of what we believed was a little girl, lost during the first trimester of pregnancy. Nora talked with her doctor, and he recommended that she light a candle, fill a special box, say a prayer—in some way honor this brief life. Nora selected a decorative box and each family member prepared something to add to the box, with love: a poem, a partially knitted blanket, a favorite toy, a pocketknife, a note, and so on. Nora and I had a memorial service with just our children. We cried as we shared what had been our hopes and dreams for this child's life. (That service took me back to the pain of losing our unborn baby when Jenny died.) Nora wrote this poem for our miscarried child:

"Ilana Lee?"

The highs. The lows.
Of what no longer grows.
The meals. The flowers.

A Widower's Walk

Sympathy calls.
Make sweet, sad hours.
The highs. The lows.
Of what now newly rose.
Never born. Yet reborn.
And who could be forlorn?
Surrounded by
such caring eyes, words,
prayers, gestures.
A surprise.
Surprised by joy. By grief.
By pain. Fainting. Relief.
What flows besides the blood?
But love in grief.
Our brethren with us mourn
a life too brief.

Elnora Lee White

    Toward the end of my assignment with Manpower & Reserve Affairs, I was blessed to be promoted to lieutenant colonel. I treasure the pictures made during the promotion ceremony. Wearing my service "A" uniform, I knelt down so that Nora, Hannah, Ethan, Lydia, and Ian could pin my new rank on my coat's shoulder epaulettes, shirt collar, and cover (hat). One Marine commented that he thought it was cool that I had not done the typical pinning-on part of the promotion ceremony by standing at attention, but rather had knelt down so my wife and children could reach my uniform and pin on the new rank insignia.

In 2007, I reported to the Pentagon for duty as the Assistant Chief, Multinational Operations Division in the J-3 of The Joint Staff. This assignment allowed me to serve with many outstanding officers and civilians from Australia, Canada, France, Germany, Italy, the United Kingdom, and the United States. Nora and I were able to plan—thanks to several international officers' assistance for finding the best travel deals—our tenth anniversary celebration in Germany, Norway, and Italy. I joked with Nora that our tenth anniversary celebration was the peak of our marriage, for after that European extravaganza, all future anniversaries would be downhill!

Days before my first trip after reporting to the Pentagon, Nora and I elected for her to have an induced labor so that we could be together during her delivery of *Dash-5*. Phillip Franklin arrived mid-day in September 2007 at the Fort Belvoir military hospital. God was with us as Phillip faced severe asthma and a ride in the ambulance (a scary time for Nora as I was overseas on a temporary assignment) during his first year of life. With God's help, he outgrew those health issues so well that you wouldn't know he had been a sickly one-year-old tied to his nebulizer. With a shock of brown curls on his head and his sensitive brown eyes, Phillip lights up our world with his focus on accomplishing what he sees as his mission each day. Even as a young child, he insisted on pushing the envelope of safety as a thrill-seeker.

"Where'd You Get Your Flashing Eyes?"

*Ebony depths and pools of brown.
Sometimes warrior, sometimes clown.
Fierce as a lion, or sad as a hound.
Luminous, like liquid found,*

rolled up inside those orbs of brown.

Who could read the words unspoken?
Beneath dark lashes, brows a token~
arched around two pots of gold~
flashing secrets, warmth untold,
inside two eyes not three years old.

Elnora Lee White

In November 2008 we saw God's comfort again during another miscarriage.

"A Shiny Thing"

I lost a babe
whose God had seen
those unformed parts
inside me, gleam.
*There **was** a shine*
on Thanksgiving,
though babe had passed
to parts unseen,
in Glory Land
*there **was** a gleam.*
But not a tear,
our babe won't cry.
Yet how she seemed
(or was it he)
sealed up inside

CHAPTER OF LIFE WITH NORA BEGINS

a memory,
too small to die?
Our baby gleamed
too bright for earthly eyes.

Elnora Lee White

Just two years and two months younger than Phillip, Erik Elijah joined us early one morning in November 2009, also at the Fort Belvoir military hospital. With his fair complexion, blond hair, and bright blue eyes, Erik has charmed his way into the heart of everyone he meets. His gift of the spoken word has given him the moniker of *Silver Tongue*. He loves the outdoors and has the heart of a warrior.

"Cathedral Baby"

Every cherub in heaven
was made to look like you.
Each cathedral on earth
bears your fair image, too.
Peaches and cream,
pink roses and silk.
Skin soft as feathers,
creamy like milk.
Round as a dumpling
or a bunny rabbit's tummy.
With scowly face or scrunchy nose
you look divinely funny!

A WIDOWER'S WALK

Snuggling or struggling,
giggling or wiggling,
floating or splashing,
chattering unabashedly.
You shake your blond head
like a mangy dog
we call you "Shaggy-Woo."
Yet, all the angels in heaven,
Love, are smiling down on you.
A celestial little package
with yet a crowning glory;
The color of a perfect sky,
bright blue eyes tell the story!
So listen up, or hitch a ride.
Head toward the Sistine Chapel,
find our cherub painted there;
With wide blue eyes
and wavy lashes
and sunshine in his hair.

Elnora Lee White

CHAPTER 15

Career ~ Crash and Burn

However, even with the blessing of a beautiful wife and four boys and two girls, I was failing as a husband and a father. And the sad part was that I didn't realize it, as it occurred slowly. I began to get off course, seeking affirmation from others and recognition for my hard work in order to be selected for a command assignment. I relied on the cool story of how Nora and I met, instead of consistently nurturing our relationship and studying her more to know her better. And I began to turn into a workaholic, again, and was not at home spending time with Nora and our children. With the change of assignment to the Pentagon (and still living at Quantico), my commute changed from ten minutes across base to one and one-half hours each way—translated: fifteen hours per week commuting if all went well and there were no accidents, protests, and such. I became consumed with being selected for command of a Marine engineer unit and checking a big box on my resume in order to get promoted to Colonel—and receive another medal.

However, the wheels began to come off of my career. In 2009, exploratory arthroscopic knee surgery did not fix (with a *microfracture* technique) the years-long chronic pain in my left knee. (At that point, I had just over eighteen years of service toward a twenty-year retirement.) The surgeon discovered that I had almost no cartilage in my left knee and that arthritis was present throughout the joint. He told me a knee replacement wasn't advisable at that time because I was only 40 years old. Forty was deemed too young for a knee replacement, as the medical officials didn't believe the knee replacement would last the rest of my life. I began to see the proverbial *writing on the wall*—my career was over. Months of physical therapy didn't provide any relief to my knee pain, nor did multiple cushioning-type medications injected into my knee. Unable to run even a mile, I couldn't in good conscience ask my Marines to run if I couldn't. I tried using one of the treadmills in the Pentagon Athletic Center (PAC) for exercise but that caused pain. Next I attempted to use an elliptical machine in the PAC, but my knee continued to buckle without warning and caused me to fall off the elliptical. Not intending to provide *comedy hour* for dozens of other service members in the PAC, I quit using the PAC exercise machines. Swimming wasn't an option, due to chronic pain in both shoulders. I started walking to/from the Virginia Rail Express commuter train stop at Crystal City to the Pentagon to get to work, and that seemed bearable—if I took a host of prescribed pain medication.

  The military is a young man's *Rod and Gun Club,* and if you can't keep up, you're done. In 2010, with almost nineteen years of service, I recognized, that regardless of whether the Marine Corps retired me medically (with less than twenty years of service) or allowed me to serve until the twenty-year point, my career was over.[10] Upon this realization, I turned my back on God. I remember thinking, *My wife died; my son died; my unborn baby died . . . and now my career has died. Why should I continue*

---

10   Once a person has served twenty years of active duty in the U.S. military, he or she may retire and receive a monthly pension until his/her death.

trusting You, God? I feel like You've abandoned me. I'm out of here. I went through the motions of going to church, trying to keep up a façade for our children. But Nora kept praying for me and encouraging me—trusting that things would work out for the good.

"Marrying a Crippled Man"

Standing there. In the hall.
You didn't look crippled
then, at all.
Exchanging vows ~
for better, for worse.
God, give us better!
Move on, long dark hearse.

For richer, for poorer,
in sickness, in health.
Is your breathing machine
our last sign of wealth?
Who would've guessed
when I first held
your hand,
That I could be marrying
a crippled man?

Is it your spirit
or just a bad knee?
What part of tomorrow
might need surgery?
I stroll under blue skies

A WIDOWER'S WALK

and breathe in fresh green.
You crunch through odd numbers
and stare all night
at a screen.

Always some cause
not to swim, stroll or rise?
This ache or that pain,
this dream or that dies?
Lying beside me
a man barely forty.
Yet the cares of a lost cause
make a victor
feel thwarted.

I remember how sturdy
how ruddy and tall.
You didn't seem crippled then
there in the hall.
Or is it your heart
like a beaten-down boy,
insecure and defensive
unaware of the joy?
Just in our grasp,
hold my hand once again.
No crippling past
could destroy God's
true man.

Let me walk through

CAREER~CRASH AND BURN

*the sunrise
beside my husband.*

Elnora Lee White

In December 2010, for a belated anniversary celebration, I took Nora on a Potomac River dinner cruise. During that cool, damp evening, we walked outside on the *Odyssey's* deck and enjoyed a beautiful view. Across the water, a seemingly endless number of Christmas lights and decorations lined the Washington, D.C., shoreline. After a delicious meal indoors, we sipped coffee and reminisced about our story and our marriage. In that romantic setting, I looked deeply into Nora's eyes and lovingly asked her, "Would you do it again [meaning *marry me*]?"—I meant that as a rhetorical question, one asked solely for effect and not to elicit an answer.

(Nora's struggles in our relationship had been deep—her cries to God, loud and piercing as she walked through Quantico's woods and deserted golf course. She wanted to feel something for me, yet our relationship had been slowly dying as we created separate lives. With my commute to and from the Pentagon and my disillusionment with God, I began to unwind in the evening by surfing the web for homes, careers, investment opportunities, etc. As I avoided an emotionally intimate relationship with Nora, she began to rally herself around a group of ladies: walking buddies, breakfast/coffee pals, and Bible study partners.)

She paused at my question. *This hardly seemed the place,* she thought. Finally she replied, "Just think where we'd be if we hadn't done it? Our four lovely children [Lydia, Ian, Phillip, and Erik] wouldn't be here. And I may have never been able to call Hannah or

Ethan my own." And so she conveniently evaded the question—and gave herself some time to ponder her answer.

Nora held out hope that we needed to force a crisis in our marriage in order to face the state of our relationship. She didn't want to pretend anymore. She had a tiny spark of hope that things might get better—if we had the courage to speak the truth and change our patterns. She believed my question was worth answering though. So she came back to it one evening a week before Christmas. "The real answer to your question on the dinner cruise," she said, "is 'I don't know.' I don't know if I'd do it again."

Nora expected this answer to deeply hurt me. She was hurt to her core, from not having a more certain answer. She later reflected that the fact was—whether we'd do it again or not—<u>we</u> <u>did</u> <u>it</u>. We said our vows before God and man and had kept them. She meant to follow through with her commitment, even though our marriage hadn't gone the way she had dreamed.

I was cut to the heart and thought, *What do you mean "You don't know"!?! You got Captain White—now Lieutenant Colonel White. The only way our story would have had more flair would be if I had ridden into Fort Leonard Wood on a white horse. We were the talk of the town as a widower married his children's nanny—think <u>The Sound of Music</u> and start up the choir. We have this awesome, cool story. OK, if you don't know if you would do it again, then we're done as a couple. Anyway I'm tired of not measuring up to your unachievable standard for a husband. I've tried my best to help with housework, the children, and meeting your needs. But it seems like that's not good enough for you. And if that's the case, then we're through. I'm not going to put up with your dissatisfaction* *anymore. Your expectations for me as your husband exceed what I can give.*

That's what I thought, but didn't tell Nora. However my unspoken response, as a mixture of anger…hurt…coldness…totally disconnected emotionally…exasperated beyond measure, cut Nora to her soul.

I felt vindicated that I had given it my best with Nora and our cool story—but felt it would never be good enough for her. Her *Princess and the Pea* syndrome was unrealistic: she kept raising the bar on me with her expectations. In my insecurity, the problems in our relationship had to be her fault or the baggage she brought into our marriage from her upbringing—not my fault!

Everything I had leaned on—my marriage with Jenny, being a father to Lil Danny my namesake, and now my career in the Marine Corps and my marriage to Nora—had seemingly died and fallen apart. I didn't know what to do and felt helpless yet again. I briefly wondered if Nora and our children would be better off if I were gone and they had my life insurance money. *Maybe then Nora would finally be happy*, I mused.

A WIDOWER'S WALK

CHAPTER 16

Two Life-Changing Questions

I attended another seminar by the Rev. Ray Vander Laan (RVL). He shared a story, which God used to get my attention, leading me to encounter a *cocoon* process: recognizing that I was in several figurative prisons—from which the LORD would free me. The following was the story:

After a long day of teaching in the Galilee area of Israel, a rabbi sends his disciples home. He finally has some time to himself as he returns to his village. So he does what rabbis always do with alone time: he meditates on the day's Scripture passage and communes with God.

The rabbi is deeply lost in thought and when he reaches a fork in the road, instead of going left, to his home, he turns right. Still lost in thought, he hasn't a clue that he's going the wrong way.

Still lost in his meditation as twilight approaches, he is startled to hear a Roman sentry bark out a challenge, "Who are you, Jew? And what are you doing here?"

Looking up, the rabbi sees a Roman fort that he's never seen in his life. For once, the rabbi doesn't know what to say. "Uh … what?"

The sentry challenges him again, "Who are you? And what are you doing here?"

Quickly the rabbi collects himself and asks the sentry, "How much are you paid a week to ask me those two questions?"

The sentry, taken aback momentarily, answers, "Three denarii a week. Why do you ask?"

The rabbi responds, "I'll double your pay if you'll come and stand outside my home and ask me those two questions each morning: Who are you? And what are you doing here?"

RVL zeroed in and made it personal. He asked, "If you take away your title, your career, your bank account, your achievements, your academic degrees, and so forth—Who are you? And what are you doing here?"

I realized my honest answers to those questions were very shallow. I had been defining myself by what I did: picture the Marine Corps dress blue uniform, two rows of medals on my chest, Joint Staff Identification Badge (i.e., Pentagon assignment on The Joint Staff), and shiny lieutenant colonel rank on my collar—and I was striving for another medal and the next promotion. All of that was fading away as my knee issues prevented me from continuing to serve, take command, and pursue the next promotion.

Instead of being a *human being*, I had become a *human doing*. Throughout my life, I'd been seeking affirmation from others. Others—who can be fickle and untrustworthy, even after you give 110 percent to them.

Shortly after the RVL seminar, John Bishop forwarded R. Scott Rodin's essay entitled "Becoming a Leader of No Reputation" to me. That essay appeared in the Fall 2002 edition of the *Journal of Religious Leadership*. Rodin wrote that essay after serving as the president of Eastern Baptist Theological Seminary in Philadelphia, Pennsylvania. One line hit me like a lightning bolt: "It doesn't matter if the world knows, or sees or understands; **the**

only applause we are meant to seek is that of nail-scarred hands [emphasis mine]." Reality struck! I had been in a figurative prison, seeking applause from a finite source (people) when it could be had from the Infinite Source (God).

One week after Nora responded with the "I don't know if I'd do it again" to my question, Nora and our children drove the two-day trip to Missouri to share Christmas 2010 with her family. Nora felt she endured a scary drive, navigating our Suburban without me and through ice and snow. I spent Christmas alone in order to save my military leave for my anticipated transition (twenty-year retirement from the military) in 2011. During the days after Nora's answer—"I don't know"—I began to wrestle with options to answer this question in my mind: *How can I leave Nora and our children and not hurt any of them—or me?* I thought of one option. Then another.

After nearly a week of mulling over options, I realized that my proposal was ludicrous. If I left Nora and our children, they would be wounded for life. Some wounds never heal into scars—and I believed my leaving would create wounds that would never heal in all of us. What was I thinking? In front of God and dozens of witnesses, I had promised to remain with Nora until death parted us. Did my word and commitment mean nothing? Was I willing to throw away our story, due to my pride?

I visited my brother Jon and his wife over the New Year's holiday, and Jon challenged my thinking concerning my reaction to Nora and my thoughts about leaving her and our children.

Jon asked me, "Danny, do you think you don't have issues yourself?"

Throughout the weekend I pondered Jon's question and began to realize that I had been blaming my issues in marriage on Jenny and then Nora. I failed to consider that I might be part of the reason why our marriage was struggling. My upbringing had set the foundation for how I viewed marriage. (Later I read Milan and Kay Yerkovich's book *How We Love: Discover Your Love Style, Enhance Your Marriage*. Their research confirmed what I learned from examining my own life: there is a direct correlation between a child's upbringing and how the child will view all relationships, particularly marriage. The Yerkovichs also pointed out in Psalm 51:6 (CJB): "Still, you want truth in the inner person; so make me know wisdom in my inmost heart.")

Remembering that Nora enjoyed handwritten notes from me, I wrote her a nine-page letter, detailing my conciliatory thoughts, and asked her to forgive me. I admitted, *I don't know how to make our marriage work. Nor do I know what you were looking for in me as your husband. I've been trying to demonstrate my love for you in words and actions, but that doesn't seem to be enough for you. I've felt like you have this seemingly impossible standard you've set for your ideal husband—and I'll never measure up no matter how hard I try.*

As part of our original Christmas plan, I flew to Missouri to help Nora drive back to our home. I gave her the letter and waited for her response. Although deeply hurt by my admission of thinking about leaving her, she acted like Jesus and forgave me.

Nora then shared that it had been a strange Christmas without me. She had observed her newlywed siblings (two brothers and youngest sister) and their spouses decked out in holiday attire and had seen their baby girls, Kaya and Annika, in big bows. Nora noticed the special efforts her parents and siblings made to celebrate the *holy-day* of Christmas. She wondered: *What*

TWO LIFE-CHANGING QUESTIONS

has happened to Danny and me. He's off doing ...what?—I don't know. He didn't even call me on Christmas Day.

During one of those days during the 2010 Christmas season, Nora sat beside her dad (the consummate card player) in front of a fireplace at the Carlson's cottage and said, "I wish I could give a rip about my marriage!"

"Danny's a good man," her dad replied. "Maybe because of his background and his losses, he just doesn't have as many cards in his deck as most people do. Maybe he's offering you all he does have."

That image sank deep into Nora. She determined to be content with the cards I had to offer from the hand dealt to me. Even if I could never give Nora what she yearned for in a love relationship, she determined to accept what I could offer, and not demand what I could not give.

Nora felt as if she had been given another chance through my letter asking for her forgiveness and my admission that I didn't know how to be the husband she wanted. She then dropped a bombshell on me in response to my question of "What do we need to do?"

"We need to go to counseling," she said.

Immediately I pushed back internally and thought: *What? Counseling? No way! I'm a lieutenant colonel in the Marine Corps. I counsel people and help them get their acts together. I've got my act together!*

But she gently pressed her solution to me. Soon after we returned home to Northern Virginia from our Christmas apart and after our renewed promise to nurture and heal our relationship, Nora bumped into a friend after a ladies' luncheon.

That friend, a chaplain's wife, hugged Nora and asked how she'd been. Nora remembered her friend sharing a time when her daughter had struggled and had been caught doing wrong. Together, she and Nora had wept over that situation. Nora remembered that honest conversation, and it gave her courage. She answered, "Actually, Danny and I spent Christmas apart." Then Nora broke down crying. The chaplain's wife listened with concern and compassion and suggested that perhaps her husband could help. That chaplain, a prior-enlisted Marine, possessed wisdom and insight beyond his years.

Nora thanked her friend, yet felt hopeless. Nora didn't think I would agree to share our problems and needs with the chaplain and his wife. For many years, I had expected Nora not to share certain struggles and issues we faced with anyone. Nora felt she had no support system of people—no group of people I trusted—with which she could share.

But God and I surprised Nora. I talked with Nora about meeting with the chaplain and his wife and agreed to set a date and time. We met initially over lunch with the chaplain and his wife at their on-base home at Quantico, and the walls between Nora and me began to crack and then crumble.

I also gave Nora my blessing to share our struggles with a sister or whomever she believed she could trust. Why? Because I began to *let down my shield* and began to trust my bride.

As the day approached for Nora and me to meet with that Navy chaplain at his office on Quantico, I had to fight pride and wondering what people would think about me. It was humbling to have to tell my boss at the Pentagon that my marriage was struggling and ask him for time off during working hours in order to meet with that chaplain. It was humbling, as a senior officer, to go into that chaplain's office and admit that my marriage needed help. It was humbling to ask the chaplain to help me figure out how to save my marriage. But I wanted to save my marriage more than I wanted to save my pride. So, Nora and I met him for counseling. After a couple of weekly sessions together, I met with the chaplain one-on-one for several sessions. He helped me begin to pull at the thread of the problems in my marriage and helped me realize there were other figurative prisons I was in.

Since early in my life, I spent my efforts seeking affirmation from others in order to scratch an itch: did I measure up to my dad's standard of success as a man?

I threw myself into my high school studies and strove for academic success. I pursued that NROTC Marine-option scholarship in order to join the Marine Corps—the toughest organization I knew of—largely to prove to my father and the world that I was a man. I pushed myself for success academically and militarily at The Citadel. I married Jenny, started a family, and targeted a long career in the Marine Corps. With the chaplain's help, I realized that during my entire adult life, I had defined myself by what I did (i.e., as a U.S. Marine).

The chaplain also helped me with a corollary for the "Who are you?" and "What are you doing here?" questions. He proposed this corollary (a question that naturally follows those two other questions): "Why do you act and react the way you do?"

I slowly realized that I had never taken an objective look to recognize how I was wired and what my strengths and weaknesses were. My brother had challenged me with this question, "Do you think you don't have issues yourself?" I was insecure and always had to win the discussion—otherwise the house of cards would fall if I were proven wrong. To compound this flaw, I was hypersensitive about any constructive criticism. Talk about the *perfect storm* of a husband for Jenny and then Nora!

After another session with us, the chaplain recommended that Nora and I attend a Family Life Weekend to Remember® conference. He said we would get more done there for our relationship than in six months of counseling. (I told him later that he was wrong—the conference was like twelve months worth of counseling.)

We arranged for babysitting for a long weekend and attended the conference in Virginia Beach, Virginia, in February. For the first time in eighteen combined years of marriage (to Jenny, then to Nora), I attended my first marriage conference—a fact I deeply regret. How I wish I could get a *re-do* with those marbles.

As the weekend progressed, I let down my shield further and allowed Nora to see my heart and insecurities. Even more important, I listened to her heart rather than looked for inaccuracies in her statements (in order to point them out to her and defend myself). I learned at the conference that in trying to win the argument, I'm trying to make Nora lose—not quite the loving attitude that Jesus demonstrated toward His *Bride*, the Church. Perusing the resources at the conference, we discovered Dr. Gary Chapman's audio book entitled *The Five Love Languages*.[11]

After listening to that audio book together, I asked Nora, "What's your 'primary love language?' I don't know."

She replied, "*Quality Time.*"

I was dumbfounded to realize that Nora had not been putting me down because I wasn't measuring up to her standard. She had been trying to tell me that she appreciated my cleaning the dishes or folding laundry or helping with our children, but that what she really wanted was for me to spend time with her. If it came

---

11 Per his research and counseling experience, Dr. Chapman details the love languages as *Words of Affirmation, Quality Time, Gift Giving, Physical Touch, and Acts of Service.*

down to washing the dishes in the evening or spending time to talk with her, she wanted me to talk with her—and she would deal with the kitchen the next morning. In other words, I had been giving her *Acts of Service* and expecting her to receive—and even demanding that she receive—that as love, when her primary love language was *Quality Time*. Learning that was a game changer! By listening to Nora's heart through her words instead of looking for inaccuracies to zing her, I would have understood Nora's need much sooner and not have allowed her love reservoir to get dangerously empty. Demanding that Nora receive love on my terms was not love. Rather, it revealed the insecurity in me.

The puzzle pieces ("Who are you?" and "What are you doing here?") started to align for me as well, once I understood my love language: *Words of Affirmation*. I thrived my entire life with pats on the back: good grades and the subsequent accolades from my high school teachers; cadet rank and ribbons at The Citadel; a beautiful wife Jenny and incredible children: Lil Danny, Hannah, and Ethan; marrying Nora and having four amazing children with her: Lydia, Ian, Phillip, and Erik; and four promotions and fifteen medals and ribbons in the Marine Corps. I had been seeking the applause from others instead of from *the nail-scarred hands*.

After attending that first marriage conference, I committed to Nora that until either of us died, we would attend at least one marriage conference every year. I recognized that I had much to learn as a husband and father in order to teach my sons and daughters what *right* should look like. I began telling our children, the older ones in particular, about my mistakes and that the host of issues with Nora were my responsibility. I, too, had brought baggage into our marriage—and didn't recognize it. I didn't know the answer to the question: "Who are you?" And as the leader of our marriage *and* home, I—not Nora—was responsible for both nearly disintegrating.

Nora, from her perspective, felt that community was more responsible for healing our marriage (than was counseling or a conference, though both were critical). One revolving door, Nora sensed, that Satan had us trapped inside was the result of our keeping our relationship and our hearts as islands—where our secret struggles and wounds could not be touched, tended, or healed.

From that point, where I gave Nora my blessing to share our issues and struggles with those whom she trusted in our community, she felt that we were able to begin a journey toward healing through community. Not sharing everything with everyone, but being discerning and seeking God's help through others' prayer and counsel. Before either of us would ever have imagined, other couples with struggles more serious than ours began coming to us for help.

A few weeks after the Weekend to Remember® conference, I attended a start-up men's Bible study in our neighborhood located on the Marine base. We studied *Every Man's Marriage* by Stephen Arterburn and Fred Stoeker. Those authors clearly explained the biblical concept of oneness between a man and wife and shared lessons learned from their own marriages—even admitting their mistakes and struggles. I felt encouraged by their transparency and candor.

One principle in that book revolutionized my perspective as a leader in my home. Arterburn and Stoeker referred to the story of Nathan confronting David about David's sin of adultery with Bathsheba and his murder of her husband, Uriah (II Samuel 11-12). Nathan told David a parable, but David failed to see himself as a character in the parable and self-righteously demanded justice. (To a Jewish person, per RVL, when you hear a parable, you must identify yourself with one of the characters in the parable in order to have truly *heard* the parable.) Nathan told David, in essence, "You're the man who sinned. You took Uriah's only lamb (Bathsheba) when you already had other lambs (other wives)."

That challenge hit me right between the eyes: *Danny, do you see Nora as a lamb entrusted to you by God?* I had to admit that, for many years, I had not. Nor had I done so with Jenny.

I began to study the *Text* (i.e., the Bible) and listen to RVL and Dr. Pat Hayes preach and teach about shepherds. God has a shepherd's heart and demonstrates an affinity for shepherds, compared with non-shepherds, as seen in the Text. I was amazed to realize that much of biblical leadership involves *leading as a shepherd:* leading by example by walking in front of the flock, leading with voice, and being willing to lay down one's life for the sheep.

Jesus said, "I am the Good Shepherd" in John 10:11 (ESV). In essence, the Good Shepherd stays and protects His sheep. He doesn't run when the flock is attacked. I acted like a hireling and was ready to run when things got tough in my marriage with Nora.

During our 2011 anniversary celebration, I asked Nora, "Would you do it again?"

To my tremendous relief, she said, "Yes!"

Nora later shared this:

"We can wish things were different in the past, but would we risk losing what we have in the present? Before I met Danny, I was immature and too many of my ideals were influenced by the world. I'm glad I said, 'Yes,' to him. My life with Danny is God's gift to me, now, and it was God's gift to me, then, even during our desert times.

"Through our marriage, God has helped me to find my destiny within my home, to sacrifice for those I love, and to nurture those placed in my care. Jesus provided an example that all women can follow. He sacrificed His very life on the Cross just as we pour ourselves out daily for our families. Our Divine Homemaker has gone to prepare the perfect place for His family to spend eternity. I pray I can follow His lead and create a bit of heaven on earth for mine."

CHAPTER 17

Lead with Liberty Version 1.0

Reaching the end of Calling #1, as a Marine, I wrestled with possible options for Calling #2:
- Stay in the Washington, D.C. area to pursue one of many available, lucrative jobs?
- Move to the Southeast or Midwest to be near family?
- Pursue employment as a federal civilian employee in the Midwest or Southeast?
- Become an entrepreneur?

After talking with a friend, who had been my company commander during 1992-1994, about the options I was considering, he asked me, "What does Nora think about those options?" I realized my planning efforts had been a solo attempt and caused me unnecessary stress—by not seeking my bride's advice.

Nora and I, together, began weighing the options and praying. One morning during a breakfast date over pancakes, I shared with her my concerns: I was feeling as though it was impossible to determine the right job, the right home location, and the right church. She listened and then wisely stated, "Let's not try to solve everything at once. Rather, let's take one step or jump one lily pad at a time."

Wow—sheer brilliance!

Thus, we began to determine which lily pad should be first: *where* or *what* for Calling #2. I'll always remember when the first piece of the puzzle fell into place. Nora and I took a walk on the Marine base at Quantico on a crisp, clear evening in November 2011. As we held hands and talked, we discussed the *what* and *where* questions and the subsequent narrowing possibilities, as we had decided *where* was more important than *what*.

I told Nora, "I think I'd like to try something in the logistics field—maybe freight or trucking. I'm comfortable with that, based on my lessons learned and experience in the Corps." Again, relying on what felt comfortable.

After listening to my description of these possibilities and my reasoning, Nora told me, "That's not your strength. God's wired you with the heart of a teacher. So you need to do something with speaking or teaching. When I first met you in January 1998, you were speaking at the Fort Leonard Wood chapel service."

Wow! She was right again.

From that point on I did not consider anything other than speaking or consulting—and later started my own company.

We went to Missouri to share Thanksgiving 2011 with Nora's family. Driving back to Quantico, we both realized separately that we felt a tug to transition from the Corps in Virginia to Missouri. We talked about it and prayed. And prayed some more. Then we decided to rent a furnished home in Missouri for twelve months, while the preponderance of our household goods were stored by the Marine Corps for those same twelve months. That would allow us to *test drive* the area, while giving some flexibility for one last military-funded move.

After being freed from my multiple figurative prisons during Calling #1 and seeing my marriage healed and growing, I began, with excitement and passion, sharing with friends about my new vision. Three of them arranged for me to speak to men's groups in their churches in Virginia, South Carolina, and Florida. Having nearly thrown away my story of meeting Nora, I was unsure how to proceed.

Nora encouraged me to be transparent and candid.

"Many of those men will not be able to relate with what you went through in losing Jenny and Lil Danny and your unborn baby," she said. "You've lived a husband's and a parent's worst nightmare. However, if you'll let down your shield and admit your mistakes and your lessons learned, you'll relate with your audience."

Again, wise advice from my bride.

The response at the three meetings exceeded anything I had imagined. In Florida I was privileged to speak at length with a Marine wounded warrior and pray with him about PTSD concerns he had.

During spring of 2012, Nora and I met with a professional speaker to learn about the steps we should take to launch a professional speaking career for Calling #2. During that meeting, I provided an overview of my leadership journey. I described about being freed from multiple figurative prisons: being a workaholic, being worried about money, worrying about what people thought about me, defining myself by what I did, being hypersensitive about constructive criticism, and seeking affirmation from others. I mentioned that the Marine Corps foundational leadership principle—"Know yourself and seek improvement"—finally made sense … after naively missing it as a second lieutenant.

I also shared about enjoying the experience of commissioning Nora's brother Kristian into the U.S. Navy Chaplain Corps in December 2011 as we stood beside the Liberty Bell in Philadelphia.

Plus I had been unable to stop thinking about the Liberty Bell and about what it meant to our nation and about the phrase engraved on it: "Proclaim liberty throughout all the Land unto all the inhabitants thereof ~ Lev XXV X."

Then I shared a comment that John Bishop had mentioned weeks earlier.

While I was talking, during dinner with John in Alexandria, Virginia, about how God had freed me from many figurative prisons and about what He'd done in my marriage, John asked me, "Do you know why God freed you?"

"No, I don't," I said. "I've never thought about it."

"It's so you can go encourage other leaders to find their freedom in Him," John said.

After a few moments, the professional speaker told Nora and me, "You need to call your speaking business *Lead with Liberty*." Nora and I talked over this name (and *brand*) and concurred—our business was named.

"On the Precipice of a True Business"

*Steadiness and Brilliance
took flight!
When the Holy Spirit
breathed, into our
group of three,
fresh life!
Sam's brilliance
Danny's steadiness
and Nora's wings;
unite.*

> *Who are you?*
> *and What are you*
> *doing here?*
> *Lead with Liberty*
> *and you'll be soaring*
> *on new heights.*
>
> *Elnora Lee White*

After sharing a shortened version of our story at my retirement ceremony near the end of June 2012 at Henderson Hall, Arlington, Virginia, I realized that speaking was indeed what God wanted me to do for Calling #2. He then opened doors for me to speak to churches in South Carolina and Georgia while I was still on transition leave from the Marine Corps. I retired officially in October 2012 with twenty-one years, four months, and twenty days of service in the Corps.

My passion for the rest of my marbles is to be a channel, not a dam, with the lessons I learned as a Marine, husband, and father. Jesus said in John 8:36 (NKJV): "Therefore if the Son makes you free, you shall be free indeed. Then Paul wrote in Galatians 5:1 (CJB): "What the Messiah has freed us for is freedom! Therefore, stand firm, and don't let yourselves be tied up again to a yoke of slavery." Being freed to walk in liberty in my relationship with God and my wife and children far outweighs another promotion or another medal.

During Thanksgiving 2011, God gave me a picture of His blessing demonstrated in a family photo: our *tribe* surrounded Nora, and she was smiling again. When Jenny died, she and I had two boys, one girl, and one unborn baby. In that November 2011 photo, Nora and I had been blessed with four boys and two girls. A double blessing—since God said children are a blessing and a reward from Him. God is good…all the time!

And as if that were not enough, God continued to bless Nora and me. We welcomed Noel Stephen into our family early one morning in December 2012. Noel (pronounced like Joel) was our first baby not born while I served in the Marine Corps. And our white 1999 GMC Suburban was officially full. In fact we had a mechanic replace the front center console with a bench seat so that our entire tribe of nine could ride in one vehicle. We have all loved Noel with his dark brown eyes and brown curls and what seems like a big brain in his big head that's always thinking. We wonder if he'll be a wellness doctor in the future as he loves to learn about how the human body functions and how to help people.

"Our First Noel"

*Last year he was our Christmas Babe,
wrapped in "swaddling clothes,"
Mom laid him in a "manger bed"
so we could see him posed;
Beneath the twinkling Christmas tree,
the sweetest package he could be,
inspired our live nativity
(which even Dad woke up to see).
Brothers were shepherds in
brand new bathrobes,
with throw blankets draped,
for Mary and Joseph's clothes.
A cradle surrounded by stuffed animals,*

all honoring Baby's first Noel.
A whole year has passed,
will the vision hold?
Now that Noel Stephen
is twelve months old?

Twelve months worth of smiling
with round, rosy cheeks.
His fair share of howling
when siblings won't "keep the peace."
Twelve months of arched brows,
dark eyes seeming shy,
suspicious, but delicious!
Like chocolate mousse pie.
With his teensy nose
and his downy curls,
the cleft in his chin,
oh, he's king of our world!
A skeptic? A scholar?
A well-earned friend.
A baby's a person!
We've learned that from him.
An honest chap—his emotions are sure,
With his back arched in anger
or his smile, soft and dear.

A year's worth of growing,
exploring and knowing.
Learn to clap, give a kiss,
cut six teeth, climb the steps.

*No longer a babe wrapped
in swaddling clothes.
The tree is a new one,
fresh presents and bows.
But in our memory lingers
our first Christmas with Noel.*

Elnora Lee White

Yet we were amazed that God was not done blessing us with children. Elnora Christine Abigael joined us early one afternoon in October 2015. She loves her brothers and being mom's fellow female in a house filled with males. Christine is a *Daddy's girl* and reminds us much of both sisters at the same age.

"Ballad of a Sparrow"

*You look at me. Passionately.
You stare as if you know.
That eye that won't cooperate
still sees inside my soul.
It bothers me, my lovely dear,
waiting sixteen years to bring you here.
Such pretty eyes, a light brown gleam—
peevish, pensive, tender, keen.
Why must an eye behave so mean?
Why must it inward hover?
"Is that a lazy eye?",
Some ask her mother.*

LEAD WITH LIBERTY VERSION 1.0

There's nothing lazy 'bout this girl!
She's Cinderella, watch her twirl
or hum and scrub the floor for fun
or pick up things for everyone.
Oh, God, who made her honeyed curls
so downy soft, our Teeny Bird;
A mother hen to all six brothers—
meows with Noel, burping Anders.
"Hey, Boys!", she poses in her frills,
big sister's purse, her mommy's heels.
She's Daddy's Princess pouring tea
on Mor Mor's staircase, daintily.
She sings the wellness of her soul,
our Narrow Sparrow finely formed,
articulate—yet thus adorned—
with one eye drifting...heaven scorned?

Should it matter very much?
Was the Master Potter's touch
only shaky just this once?
And if shaky He had been,
can He smooth the mark and try again?
Or could it be, my Little Lamb,
your Shepherd had a different plan?
He's herding souls that go astray.
He even herds the stars in place.
If constellations keep their spot
for mariners and earth bound lot
to mark our way;
Could He not make one small eye stay?

Though her sister Leah's eyes were weak,
it wasn't Rachel's line you see,
which bore our Shepherd, Savior, King.
But it's hard to care for lofty things
when I catch your eye faltering.
Or maybe while I question why,
inside your own sweet wandering eye—
God's unseen things are passing by.

Elnora Lee White

After nearly two years of wellness therapy to address Christine's various sensory issues, we felt at peace for our daughter to undergo eye surgery. God's timing was remarkable. Just a few days after Nora wrote this poem about Christine's eyes, we met with a pediatric ophthalmologist. The doctor's gentle manner calmed Christine during pre-surgery appointments; and post-surgery, people have continued to remark about how well her eyes have adjusted.

And the Almighty was still not done with showering us with His blessings. Anders Jonathan arrived late one evening in February 2018. We marvel at his mischievous eyes and desire to be a helper to his siblings and parents. Anders loves to shadow his dad and brothers and at times seems like he's *frustrated* as a man trapped in a baby's body. Mom has enjoyed calling him *The Boy* because even though she has five other sons, he's surely one of a kind.

"Sixth Son"

Who can know the mind of Jesus?
If five sufficed,
*would **six** boys please us?*
For sixteen years Mom soldiered on,
*at **last** another girl was born.*
Just two years later held the dream,
a baby sister for Christine?
Ah, who could know the ways of Christ?
Or offer pink frills for advice,
*when He seemed to find **blue** twice as nice?*

But I digress, don't miss the fun,
that followed Anders Jonathan!
When Jesus closed door #1,
He burst through a window with this son:
Sharing Ethan's blond curls,
Ian's sports loving show,
the daring of Phillip,
Erik's cherubic glow,
Noel's concentration,
three sisters' adoration…
*God **still** broke the mold.*

With irrepressible Anders J.
nursery workers (and Mom)
unite to say,
"That cutie is a thunderbolt!"
Energy in constant motion

interrupted only by a "sleeping potion."
Until once again those baby blues scan
something new to conquer,
wriggling out of our hands.
Eyes sparked with mischief and desire,
Stocky legs dash like a force on fire,
(A double portion of guardian angels required).

"'Course He isn't safe. But He's good..."*
Ah, who predicts God's ways,
who could?
Fifth son and done? Touché!
Or there'd have been no Anders J.

Elnora Lee White

(*Mr. Beaver describes Aslan in C.S. Lewis' <u>The Lion, the Witch and the Wardrobe</u>*)*

Conclusion

So, Friend, my hope is that you've taken time to consider the concept of leading with liberty—and are experiencing the inner freedom to lead yourself well. I hope you've wrestled with whether or not you're in one or more of the figurative prisons I found myself in.

- Being a workaholic…putting your to-do list before relationships.
- Having become a human *doing* rather than a human *being*.
- Lacking a spirit of generosity with your time and money.
- Being more concerned about other people's opinion rather than the *applause of the nail-scarred hands*.
- Blaming the problems in your relationships, particularly in your marriage, on others.

My hope for you is that once you understand how to lead yourself with liberty and have been freed from any prisons of insecurity, you may lead others with liberty.

- Let your shield down and listen so that others can see your heart.
- Take ownership of your baggage and how you're wired.
- Cease always having to be right in discussions.
- Learn how those you are privileged to lead receive love.
- And lead like a shepherd—putting the needs of those you lead before yourself.

Also, I wish it were possible to give you a marble to carry with you in your pocket or purse—as a reminder that today is precious. Time is the most valuable resource you have.

Why?

Please come with me to this scene: Nora, our children, and I drove up the driveway to my parents' home. However, this time was different. My 68-year-old mother—my number one cheerleader since 1969—was not sitting in her rocking chair on the front porch and looking out at the Blue Ridge Mountains while awaiting our arrival. Why wasn't she there? We had just returned from her funeral—she had suffered from a lingering illness and died a few days after Thanksgiving 2012. The house seemed but a shell of what it was when Mama was alive.

Fifty days later the scene was repeated, but it was different. What was the difference? We returned from my 41-year-old brother's funeral. He died unexpectedly from a heart attack just after New Year's Day 2013. Jon was my best male friend; I learned much from his study of the Bible and frequently sought his Solomonic wisdom as we talked several times each week.

My mother and brother's deaths rocked my world, again, and I felt the hurt, the heat, and the helplessness of the desert again. I felt as if something broke inside me upon hearing that my brother died … as grief compounded on itself. It seemed as if two pillars had been knocked out of my life.

In spending time with God and seeking His comfort and help, I felt the LORD gently encouraged me to lean on Him—to allow Him to be the pillars in my life that Mama and Jon had been. Yet again, I was reminded of several previous lessons learned, and new ones too. Each day, I want to ask myself, "How am I using today's marble?"

CONCLUSION

For none of us knows when we'll reach the last marble in our jars—Mama and Jon didn't know.

My mother and brother's deaths reminded me of my own mortality and my need for community. After I sent an e-mail to friends and family (my community), letting them know about my mom's death and weeks later my brother's death, they responded with gracious words and prayers, which God used to comfort and strengthen me and keep me running my race.

Having begun to understand the life-changing questions—*Who are you?* and *What are you doing here?*—I was reminded that no one can make it through life's deserts on his/her own. For in the desert we find an environment in which none of us will survive alone. The adversity—the heat of the day, extreme thirst, and the desert's frigid nights—will kill us.

I need God and the community He's placed in my life at all times, particularly during the tough times…when you gain a "*Purple Heart* of suffering." I thank Him for being with us, His children, in the deserts. For the deserts are where we learn about God and where our relationships with Him can go to higher levels than ever before experienced on our faith journeys. When those desert experiences come, and they will, don't be too quick to get out of the heat. It is in the fire that we are refined. When we are in pain, if we tune out the noise of the world, read His Word, and spend time praying, God will speak to us in the quiet. And I think He might say this: *I'm with you. You are not alone. My grace is sufficient*—for the "marble" you've been given today.

Soli Deo Gloria! ("To God Alone Be the Glory!")

"A Widower's Walk"

A journey without warning.
An evening without morning.
A song without a dance.
A life with no last chance.
A sob without a sound.
A clock that spins around.
Where will it stop?
This loneliest walk?
How will it end?
Holding hands with the Savior.
Face to face with a Friend.

Elnora Lee White
(inspired by the story in this book)

Postscript ~ Lead with Liberty Version 2.0

From 2012 to 2019, I ran Lead with Liberty as a business with a limited liability company (LLC) format. There were multiple opportunities, in both faith-based and non-faith-based settings, to present this story to encourage others along their leadership journeys.

Yet, I struggled to find traction from year to year in booking consistent speaking engagements along with income to provide for my family. Numerous individuals told me, "Danny, you have a powerful story, and people need to hear it. So many in the world don't have hope. Your story provides hope and encouragement."

Thus, I focused on building my network by participating in leadership forums, meeting key decision makers, and providing leadership and resiliency training and speeches. Yet, it didn't seem to *move the needle* resulting in more speaking opportunities.

Then in 2017, 2018, and again in 2019, I wrestled with wanting to quit Lead with Liberty but felt that I would be out of step with the LORD. Nor would I be demonstrating perseverance and endurance along my journey. (When asked to return to speak for a church or business, I had developed a talk about persevering through tough times in life, using the Marine Corps endurance course as the skeleton of the talk. Then I shifted the talk to biblical examples of those who endured uncertain and difficult times.)

God challenged me about quitting Lead with Liberty—that I would be in essence saying *Do what I say... not what I do*. Gulp.

Okay, LORD, I'll stick with Lead with Liberty.

I knew that God wanted me to start the LLC in late 2011/early 2012, and Nora was on board supporting this effort. I didn't want to abandon Lead with Liberty and disobey the LORD. Yet, I knew that the Bible directs that I must provide for my family—and Lead with Liberty was not bringing in the income I needed to care for my family.

In April 2019, I put two *fleeces* before God, seeking His guidance. Two organizations had expressed interest in my speaking for them. I asked the LORD, *Please have these organizations contact me by June 30, 2019, if You want me to continue with Lead with Liberty full time (i.e., as an entrepreneur). If I don't hear from them by June 30th, then I'm going to take it that You are okay with my pursuing full-time employment.*

At the end of June 2019, I would have been in business for seven years. I knew that the number *seven* is significant in God's Word as it represents "completion" or "perfection." Perhaps Lead with Liberty being in business for seven years was the completion of this season.

I talked this over with my wife Nora, and she counseled me not to apply for full time work until July 1st. She advised me not to get ahead of God or try to jump start the process.

June 30th came and went with neither organization asking me to speak for them. Acknowledging Nora's wisdom, I began applying for full time employment after July 1, 2019.

I applied for three full time positions that summer. With two of these jobs, I was referred to the hiring manager as a fully qualified candidate. Yet neither organization made a job offer. I was frustrated and confused—that perhaps I had lost the edge of being value-added since I had retired from the military seven years ago.

In early 2019, my friend Mike Osterhoudt asked me to consider serving as the speaker for his church's men's retreat. I talked it over with Nora, and she felt that I should accept—even though it would mean my departure flight from Missouri would be on our 21st anniversary.

In coordinating the administration and logistics, the church offered a generous honorarium. I realized that my expenses would make a significant dent in the amount of the honorarium—reducing what I'd have to provide for my family.

Initially, I thought about seeking a larger honorarium. Yet after talking with Nora then a friend (an Army chaplain), they both advised me separately just to accept what was offered. In essence, if you value the friendship with Mike—rather then more money—just accept what's been offered and trust God. I agreed with their advice and accepted the offered honorarium and purchased my airline tickets.

In September 2019, I flew to Northern Virginia to speak for the men's retreat—entitled *Break Through*. For several years, Mike and I had attempted to make this happen, but it hadn't worked out. We recognized that 2019 was when God wanted it to happen.

Friday morning before we departed for the men's retreat, Mike, his wife Deborah, and I were eating breakfast and sharing updates from our lives. Deborah asked me if I was on any social media. I replied that I had left social media in early 2019, for neither of the platforms I was on had generated any speaking engagements—plus, I didn't really care to know what someone's cat had eaten for breakfast.

Deborah gently counseled me that people today are on social media and that, if I wanted to get the Lead with Liberty message out, I needed to *go* where people are. Knowing Deborah to be a wise, godly lady, I recognized that I should consider her advice. I agreed to *consider* re-engaging with social media—but anticipated that I would decide not to do so.

Mike and I departed for his church to pick up two more men—one of whom was Gary Keys—then we drove to the Christian conference center in West Virginia. En route, Gary shared his testimony of God calling him and his wife Lisa from Ireland to the United States to serve essentially as missionaries. Gary had been serving at Mike's church for several years and had helped Mike in planning and coordinating Break Through as well as previous men's retreats.

We checked in to the conference center and found everything running smoothly. I went to my room to prepare and go through my Friday evening talk of "Biblical Endurance for Men" one more time. All of us men met for supper then moved back to the meeting room.

After speaking that evening and having a question and answer (Q&A) session, I met with some of the men on the retreat planning team and was overwhelmed with their feedback. Gary told me that, in several years of helping with men's retreats, he had never seen the men sit still for a speaker. He related that they would get up to get coffee or a drink, talk to each other, use the men's room, etc. But only two of the men got up while I was speaking…and that was to get a pen to take notes.

I was humbled with that feedback and blessed God for this opportunity to partner with Him and encourage these men to pursue *break through* in their lives.

Saturday morning I shared Part 1 of my story (the deaths of Jenny, Lil Danny, and our unborn baby) with another Q&A session. After lunch, there were several activities to help the men to bond together. Saturday evening I shared Part 2 of my story (God freeing me from multiple figurative prisons) and sensed God not wanting me to have a Q&A session—rather let the men process the lessons learned which the LORD had taught me.

Saturday evening, Gary and I started talking around 11:00 PM... and didn't stop until 2:00 AM Sunday morning. I shared my heart with him: my frustration and disappointment with where Lead with Liberty was at and the significant difference of where I had hoped it would be after seven years of being in business. While I don't remember everything we talked about, I know that God spoke through Gary to me: *Shut down Lead with Liberty Version 1.0 as a business / LLC and re-form it as Version 2.0 as a ministry / 501(c)(3).* Then Gary strongly encouraged me to get back on social media.

I felt like a boulder rolled out of my rucksack. I no longer had to figure out how to be a successful businessman post-Marine Corps.

After Gary and I parted ways, I went to my room but was too excited to sleep. I began researching what exactly a 501(c)(3) organization was, how to set one up, etc. After an hour or so, I unwound enough to go to sleep.

A few hours later, I woke up and was getting ready for speaking during the last session about "Shepherd Leadership." I sensed the LORD speaking to me. *Give away the books you brought to the retreat.*

I replied, *But, LORD, that's $251.10 that I'm giving up.*

God spoke again: *Give away the books you brought.*

I knew that it was the LORD speaking and remembered that Nora had not felt comfortable selling books at ministry events on Sunday—even though I had resisted her input and sought approval from pastors before selling books at ministry events. I knew that what Nora had sensed was in alignment with what God was directing at Break Through.

In my heart, I replied *Okay, LORD. I'll give the books away. But there was one man who bought two books last night with his credit card. I've never processed a credit card refund with my mobile device.*

The LORD spoke, *Well, you have cash. Give him a refund with cash.*

I replied, *Okay, LORD. I will do that.* I then refunded the man his book purchase price before the worship time.

After standing up to speak, I became very emotional, feeling awestruck by encountering God just hours before and His giving me *break through* in my life.

I told the men that I had showed up to the men's retreat expecting to partner with God and to encourage them to realize break through in their lives. Little did I expect to encounter God and see break through in my own life.

Continuing, I asked them to forgive me if I came across as manipulative Saturday evening after I shared Part 2 of my story—when I had asked them to consider purchasing a book.[12]

I told the men that I was taking my first baby step in ministry. If any of them wanted a book, then take one after the session was over.

Afterwards, I looked at the back table and all the remaining books were gone.

---

12   The retreat planning team had planned for 80 men to attend the retreat. Only 50 showed up. I wanted the 30 men who didn't attend to be able to read about God's faithfulness to me during tough times as well as the figurative prisons from which He had freed me. Saturday evening I asked the men to consider purchasing a book to give a man who hadn't attended the retreat.

I started shaking hands with the men and listening to their feedback and life stories. After shaking hands with one man, I looked down in my palm and saw a $50 bill. My heart was overflowing with gratitude: *Thank You, LORD, for providing.*

After returning from lunch—the last event of the retreat—I returned to the conference room to pick up my suitcase and computer bag. I was stunned to find two $100 bills lying on my suitcase. I found a $20 bill lying under a blank piece of paper by my computer bag.

Bottom line: the LORD provided, through the men's generosity, $330 in cash. Wow! He surpassed what I would have received by trying to sell the books.

After we departed from the conference center, someone gave a generous donation, which covered my airline tickets.

Monday morning, Gary took me to Washington Dulles International Airport for my return flight to Missouri. We loaded the plane on time, pushed away from the gate…then sat on the tarmac for over an hour waiting for approval to take off.

I texted Nora to let her know that likely I would not make it home that night since it was highly probable I'd miss the connecting flight from St. Louis Lambert International Airport to the Waynesville-St Robert Regional Airport on post at Fort Leonard Wood. Therefore, I'd have to overnight in St. Louis.

Due to the long delay in departing Dulles, I did arrive at the St. Louis airport too late to make the connecting flight to Fort Leonard Wood. Plus, my luggage was missing in action when I landed. I filed a report with the airline's baggage claim office along with my cell number. They assured me that they would call my cell if my luggage arrived that evening.

I found a hotel that offered a courtesy shuttle to/from the airport—to avoid an expensive taxicab ride. While riding to the hotel, the van driver and I started talking. She said, "Someone bought me this pizza, but I don't care for the toppings. Would you like it?"

I offered to pay her for it, but she wouldn't accept any money. So God provided my supper that evening.

When we reached the hotel and I was getting my computer bag, I sensed the LORD speaking, *Give her a tip…a generous one.*

I pulled a $20 bill from my wallet and gave it to the driver. She said, "Sir, that's too much. You don't have to do that. I usually only get a couple of dollars."

I replied, "Ma'am, God's been generous to me and blessed me. I want to bless you." Her face lit up with the biggest smile.

The next morning, after getting a courtesy shuttle ride back to the St. Louis airport, I returned to the airline's baggage claim office to see if my luggage had arrived yet. They said that it hadn't, but they would check their luggage tracking system. They then were surprised to see that a flight was arriving from Atlanta with my bags.

I returned to the airline's baggage claim office, with my luggage, to close out my missing baggage claim. To my surprise, they provided a $150 voucher for future airline travel since I had picked up my bags, and they didn't have to deliver them to my home address.

So God kept blessing and blessing and blessing…far exceeding the $251.10 I would have made selling books.

As 2019 merged into 2020 then 2021, we began transitioning Lead with Liberty from Version 1.0 (business) to Version 2.0 (ministry). While I don't know exactly what Lead with Liberty Version 2.0 will look like in seven years, I know that the LORD will provide for us as we speak and share lessons learned with those who are in need of encouragement.

In continuing to give books away at speaking events, I've been amazed to see the number of books that were picked up and how the donations exceeded what the sales revenue would have been.

I shared this with Gary Keys and he related an amazing story of God providing for a friend of his. God had told Gary's friend to open a Christian bookstore.

After a year or so of being in business, the friend had approached the LORD seeking guidance. *LORD, I opened the store like You told me to. But it's not making the revenue I need to care for my family.*

He sensed God replying *I never told you to put in a cash register. Take out the cash register and put a donation box by the front door. And trust Me.*

The friend obeyed and took out the cash register and put a donation box by the front door. Within the first week of doing this, he received more money than he had the entire previous year.

The LORD came back to him, *You have resources that people need. Let them take the books and other items, and trust Me to touch their hearts to donate.*

This story truly resonated with me in how I want to operate Lead with Liberty Ministries (i.e., Lead with Liberty Version 2.0). God has been generous and faithful to my family and me. He has provided through tough times and been a help and an encouragement. Thus, I want to freely offer this story and lessons learned to help and encourage others. God alone is my provider.

Money is no longer the driving force for me. And I feel that I've been freed from another figurative prison. After further reflection, it seems to me that *leading with liberty* is more of a process rather than a one-time event.

I bless God for being the source of liberty for all of us. For again, as Jesus said in John 8:36 (CJB), "So if the Son frees you, you will really be free!" I pray that you have found this freedom in Jesus Christ—and if you have not that you will. You will never be the same…trust me…and you will not want to go back to what you used to be.

Nora wrote this poem November 30, 2020 while reflecting on all that had passed in the years of our marriage up to that moment. She was sitting on a window seat near our wood stove observing a remarkable tree.

Later, we discussed the poem's meaning, and Nora helped me understand the different layers. (I needed a lot of help…likely much more than you would need gentle reader.)

After my *Aha* moment, discovering that the tree indeed represented me, she said with a smile, "We've come a long way, Baby—I'm forever thankful to God that *you're the one!*"

"You're the One"

In a sky of empty trees–
You're the One,
Scarlet and gold,
Still clinging to his leaves.

Nearest to my window sill–
Dearest form,
Your stalwart will
holds trembling gems,

not one shall spill.

*Were I, a bird–
and you, a tree–
Eternal Autumn
it would be.*

Elnora Lee White

And again…***Soli Deo Gloria!*** ("To God Alone Be the Glory!")